CRIME SCENE INVESTIGATIONS CRIME SCENE INVESTIGATIONS CRIM

Criminal Profiling

Searching for Suspects

I0867864

By Christine Honders

Portions of this book originally appeared in
Criminal Profiling by Jenny MacKay.

LUCENT
PRESS

Published in 2018 by
Lucent Press, an Imprint of Greenhaven Publishing, LLC
353 3rd Avenue
Suite 255
New York, NY 10010

Designer: Deanna Paternostro
Editor: Siyavush Saidian

Library of Congress Cataloging-in-Publication Data

Names: Honders, Christine, author.
Title: Criminal profiling : searching for suspects / Christine Honders.
Description: New York : Lucent Press, [2018] | Series: Crime scene investigations | Includes bibliographical references and index.
Identifiers: LCCN 2017039635 | ISBN 9781534561748 (library bound book) | ISBN 9781534562721 (paperback)
Subjects: LCSH: Criminal behavior, Prediction of–Juvenile literature. | Criminal psychology–Juvenile literature. | Criminal investigation–Juvenile literature. | Forensic sciences–Juvenile literature.
Classification: LCC HV8073.5 .H66 2018 | DDC 363.25/8–dc23
LC record available at https://lccn.loc.gov/2017039635

Printed in the United States of America

CPSIA compliance information: Batch #CW18KL: For further information contact Greenhaven Publishing LLC, New York, New York at 1-844-317-7404.

Please visit our website, www.greenhavenpublishing.com. For a free color catalog of all our high-quality books, call toll free 1-844-317-7404 or fax 1-844-317-7405.

Contents

Foreword

For decades, popular television programs and movies have depicted the life and work of police officers, detectives, and crime scene investigators. Many of these shows and films portray forensic scientists as the brains responsible for cracking cases and bringing criminals to justice. Undoubtedly, these crime scene analysts are an important part in the process of crime solving. With modern technology and advances in forensic analysis, these highly trained experts are a crucial component of law enforcement systems all across the world.

Police officers and detectives are also integral members of the law enforcement team. They are the ones who respond to 911 calls about crime, collect physical evidence, and use their high level of training to identify suspects and culprits. They work right alongside forensic investigators to figure out the mysteries behind why a crime is committed, and the entire team cooperates to gather enough evidence to convict someone in a court of law.

Ever since the first laws were recorded, crime scene investigation has been handled in roughly the same way. An authority is informed that a crime has been committed; someone looks around the crime scene and interviews potential witnesses; suspects are identified based on evidence and testimony; and, finally, someone is formally accused of committing a crime. This basic plan is generally effective, and criminals are often caught and brought to justice. Throughout history, however, certain limitations have sometimes prevented authorities from finding out who was responsible for a crime.

There are many reasons why a crime goes unsolved: Maybe a dead body was found too late, evidence was tampered with, or witnesses lied. Sometimes, even the greatest technology of the age is simply not good enough to process and analyze the evidence at a crime scene. In the United States during the 20th century, for example, the person responsible for the infamous Zodiac killings was never found, despite the earnest efforts of hundreds of policemen, detectives, and forensic analysts.

In modern times, science and technology are integral to the investigative process. From DNA analysis to high-definition surveillance video, it has become much more difficult to commit a crime and get away with it. Using advanced computers and immense databases, microscopic skin cells from a crime scene can be collected and then analyzed by a forensic scientist, leading detectives to the home of the culprit of a crime. Dozens of people work behind the scenes of criminal investigations to figure out the unique and complex elements of a crime. Although this process is still time-consuming and complicated, technology is constantly improving and adapting to the needs of police forces worldwide.

This series is designed to help young readers understand the systems in place to allow forensic professionals to do their jobs. Covering a wide range of topics, from the assassination of President John F. Kennedy to 21st-century cybercriminals, these titles describe in detail the ways in which technology and criminal investigations have evolved over more than 50 years. They cite eyewitnesses and experts in order to give a detailed and nuanced picture of the difficult task of rooting out criminals. Although television shows and movies add drama to the crime scene investigation process, these real-life stories have enough drama on their own. This series sticks to the facts surrounding some of the highest-profile criminal cases of the modern era and the people who work to solve them and other crimes every day.

Introduction

Criminal Profiling—Linking Evidence, Behavior, and Crime

In November of 1980, the bodies of four women were found around the San Francisco Bay Area. The local Federal Bureau of Investigation (FBI) worked for months to find the killer with no success, so they asked for help from FBI special agent John E. Douglas. After examining the evidence, he made a speech to the task force that was about the serial killer. He told them the killer was white, in his early 30s, and had probably spent some time in jail for sex crimes. He was shy but intelligent and probably worked in an industrial job. Douglas suspected that he may have a background in arson or was cruel to animals. "Another thing," he told his listeners, "the killer will have a speech impediment."[1]

John E. Douglas was a professional criminal profiler, and his job was to study the evidence to learn more about the specific traits of the killer and what may have motivated him. Douglas explained that since the killer used quick, brutal force on his victims, he probably had some sort of mental block that made him embarrassed to talk to them. The killer was strong, so Douglas did not think he was physically disabled, and the few eyewitnesses there were did not mention any strange physical features on the attacker. Douglas thought that the disability was something less obvious. "I may be wrong about some things," he claimed. "I may miss the age. I may miss the occupation or the IQ. But I'm certainly not going to miss the race or the sex, and ... I'm not going to miss that he has some kind of defect that really bothers him. Maybe it's not a speech impediment, but I think it is."[2]

Based at least partially on the

David Carpenter, shown here, murdered 10 women. Criminal profiling played an important part in bringing him to justice.

information detailed by Douglas and the criminal profiling team involved with the case, the killer was finally caught. In 1981, David Carpenter, the Trailside Killer, was caught and convicted of these brutal murders. He was white, had a criminal record involving sex crimes, and suffered from a severe stutter. Douglas was completely correct in all of his guesses except for age—Carpenter was in his 50s, not 30s—and he had proven how important criminal profiling is in the world of criminology.

Chapter One

The Art of Criminal Profiling

It is nearly impossible for one person to solve a crime alone. It is even more difficult in the case of a serial criminal, when it is unlikely that the victim knows the suspect. In these cases, law enforcement will create a task force of professionals all focused on solving that case. Criminal profilers are often called on to be part of that force.

Criminal profiling combines psychology, which is the study of the human mind and behavior, with forensic science, which is the application of science for the purpose of solving crimes. A profiler carefully examines the crime scene and tries to figure out what patterns exist—from the way the victims are positioned to the killer's method of murder—that might tell them something about the suspect. They develop a description, or profile, of the killer that includes behaviors and personality traits as well as age, physical description, or location. "In some ways, [profiling] is really still as much an art as a science,"[3] said psychologist Harvey Schlossberg, PhD, former director of psychological services for the New York Police Department.

The Darkest Side of Crime

In 2002, someone was shooting people at various locations near Interstate 95 from Maryland to Virginia with a powerful sniper rifle. Unsuspecting people were getting shot and killed in parking lots and at gas stations. No one knew where the next target was, and the frightened public looked to law enforcement with high expectations. With every new murder, the police seemed to be failing at their job of keeping the community safe.

This is the type of case in which profilers specialize. Serious crimes, generally involving violence or murder, and serial crimes, which are crimes committed over and over by the same person or people, are where profilers are the most help. In many ways, they dive into the darkest side of crime. They are called in for some of the most gruesome and brutal cases. The work of criminal profilers is often key to making an arrest.

"Criminal profiling," explained Gregg O. McCrary, an expert in criminology, "may be defined as 'a process used to analyze a specific crime or series of crimes in order to develop a behavioral composite of an unknown offender.'"[4] Essentially, he wrote, "the method and manner in which a crime is committed reflects an offender's personality traits. Thus, through thorough and accurate assessment of those details, we can draw certain logical inferences [assumptions] about the offender."[5]

Criminal profilers give police departments a guide for where to look. They suggest what kind of person most likely committed the crime, and they might also be able to guess where and when the criminal will strike again. They do this by utilizing theories of behavioral psychology. "The reason for many local agencies requesting a criminal profile is to help focus the investigation and perhaps narrow down the pool of suspects,"[6] McCrary wrote.

Words such as "perhaps" and "maybe" are typical in most profilers' reports. This, paired with the fact that the profiling technique is relatively new compared to other crime-solving methods makes many people question the value of profiling. If it does not lead to facts, or a definite answer, some ask if it is really forensic science. Many professional profilers say their job is a mix of science, skill, instinct, and experience. Historically, professional profilers have been quite accurate in the assessments they provide to law enforcement.

Such was the case in the first modern criminal profile, when one psychiatrist came up with a list of characteristics so similar to those of the criminal in question that it convinced the FBI to create a special department just for criminal profilers.

Introducing Psychology to Criminology

For 16 years during the 1940s and 1950s, a serial bomber was at work, detonating more than 30 bombs in crowded, busy areas of New York City, such as Radio City Music Hall and Grand Central Station. Explosion after explosion, he slipped through investigators' hands. The bomber

Occupation: Supervisory Special Agent

Job Description:
Criminal profilers working for the FBI are given the title of supervisory special agent. They are employed by the National Center for the Analysis of Violent Crime (NCAVC) and work in one of five Behavioral Analysis Units (BAU). They work alongside law enforcement agencies around the world to examine and review crime scene evidence, develop profiles of unknown criminals, assist with investigations, and help police and prosecutors determine the motive in a particular crime.

Education:
Supervisory special agents are required to have a bachelor's degree and complete a challenging training program at the FBI Academy in Quantico, Virginia. Agents applying for the NCAVC typically also have a graduate degree in behavioral or forensic science.

Qualifications:
An applicant must have at least three years of experience as an FBI special agent in addition to at least three years of field experience before applying to become a supervisory special agent. Applicants must also be between 23 and 36 years old, have outstanding vision, and be in good health. Positions with the NCAVC are extremely competitive, so candidates should have considerable experience investigating violent crime, as well as strong verbal and written communication skills.

Salary:
The average salary for a supervisory special agent in 2015 was $63,595.

came to be known as the Mad Bomber, one of the most destructive criminals of the 20th century.

Dr. James Brussel, who had studied the teachings of famed psychoanalyst Sigmund Freud, believed the Mad Bomber was leaving behind more clues than the police had been able to see. While law enforcement officers sifted through physical evidence at the scenes of the bomber's attacks, Brussel turned his attention to the bomber himself. Looking at patterns of behavior that were evident from the growing number of crime scenes, Brussel came up with a list of characteristics and traits that would most likely be present in the

George Metesky planted bombs all around New York City for 16 years, injuring 15 people. He was eventually sent to a mental institution.

Mad Bomber. He guessed at the man's race, age, weight, and religion.

Brussel came up with details about the bomber's personality and how he probably treated other people. He described a man who likely lived in one of three states—Connecticut, New Hampshire, or Maine—with one of his siblings. He even predicted how the Mad Bomber preferred to dress, going so far as to state that he would probably be wearing a buttoned, double-breasted suit when he was finally arrested. It was a long list of surprisingly specific details, and it was probably the first official criminal profile to be used in solving a crime.

George Metesky was finally identified by police and arrested in 1957 in Connecticut (one of the three states Brussel had named) in a home he shared with his two sisters. "When the police finally tracked down George Metesky," McCrary wrote, "he was in his robe, so they requested he get dressed. He came out buttoning up a double-breasted suit, just as Brussel had predicted. Most of his other details checked out as well. It was impressive."[7]

For perhaps the first time in history, a new crime-fighting tool had been used to track down a criminal—the psychological profile became national news overnight. "A psychiatrist usually studies a person and makes reasonable predictions about how that person may react to a specific situation and about what he or she may do in the future," one expert wrote. Profilers, on the other hand, work "to reverse this process. Instead, by studying an individual's deeds one deduces [concludes] what kind of person the individual might be."[8]

Criminal Profiling and Law Enforcement

Brussel's extremely accurate profile convinced the FBI that psychology was a valuable tool for solving crime. In 1972, the FBI created the Behavioral Science Unit, or BSU. At the time, the unit had only a few agents, and it was run from a small area of the FBI headquarters in Quantico, Virginia. Those early official profilers were like a new secret weapon in solving the worst crimes being committed in America—including serial murders.

Only a handful of agents worked for the BSU in its early years—but not because there was a lack of people interested. The BSU painstakingly chose and personally trained its own agents, who were investigators with the right experience and a special knack for reading the behavior of the pathological criminals who hurt and kill again and again. "Profiling violent crimes and their perpetrators is not an easy task," Deborah Schurman-Kauflin wrote. "Profiling begins with raw emotion because feeling is what drives serial behavior."[9]

Criminal profiling is more of a calling than just a job. Not all who claim the title of profiler are genuine. The true experts at this difficult form of investigation are an elite group; they must have a strong education, years of on-the-job experience, and a special ability to read and decipher the actions of criminals.

By the Numbers

36

number of serial murderers interviewed by BSU agents between 1976 and 1979

The Personality of a Profiler

Because a certain amount of guesswork goes into every criminal profile (Even expert profilers admit this.), many people believe that anyone with good intuition or feelings about people could make a decent profiler. Movies and television have helped spread this myth by simplifying the process so an audience can understand it. Regardless, the FBI handpicks its profilers for good reason. A special combination of training and a lot of experience is needed for a good profiler.

The right personality is a factor, too. The subject matter they study is among the most gruesome of any job in the world. Each day, they look at pictures of dead or injured human bodies and read graphic reports of crimes so violent that most of the details are carefully kept out of the news. These are the rare investigators who can distance themselves from the very darkest side of human nature,

Mark Hilts (left) and Susan Kossler (right) are two FBI agents who work for the Behavioral Analysis Unit (BAU), which grew out of the BSU.

Jack the Ripper

One of the most notorious serial killers in history was Jack the Ripper, who brutally murdered five women in London's East End in between August and November of 1888. He was never caught, and speculation about the identity of the murderer continues to this day.

In 1998, the FBI created a profile of Jack the Ripper. They said that Jack was an opportunistic killer, choosing sex workers in early hours of the morning because they were generally drunk and vulnerable. They also believe that his mother may have been an alcoholic and that the killer mutilated his victims because of the anger he felt toward her.

A geographical profile that was done in the 2000s pinpointed Jack's home to be within 1 square mile (2.6 sq km) of the murders. In 2006, Scotland Yard investigators gave a physical description of Jack the Ripper: 25 to 35 years old with a medium, stocky build. They also included in his profile that he would not look like an insane murderer—rather, they claimed, he would have looked quite average.

The public was very critical of the police's inability to catch Jack the Ripper. This cartoon was published in a magazine in the late 1800s.

finding valuable clues underneath all the blood, gore, and horror.

"Investigators traditionally have learned profiling through brainstorming, intuition, and educated guesswork," Douglas wrote. "Their expertise is the result of years of accumulated wisdom, extensive experience in the field, and familiarity with a large number of cases."[10]

Specialists in profiling are sometimes psychologists or psychiatrists who received law enforcement training to apply their knowledge of human behavior to criminal investigation. Alternatively, former FBI Supervisory Special Agent and BAU Chief Mark Hilts says about half of his agents are former police officers who have completed extra training in studying the human mind. Either way, profilers have many years of experience and education in crime investigations.

Professional versus Amateur Profilers

According to Schurman-Kauflin, all professional profilers have a particular set of essential skills and knowledge. First, they study many crimes. Profilers are able to create accurate profiles because they have seen or read about similar crimes before. It is an occupation that depends on studying and remembering vast amounts of detail. Qualified profilers typically have an advanced degree in criminal justice or psychological science, are trained and mentored by other expert profilers, and have firsthand experience tracking down serial criminals and talking to those who have already been caught.

"Many people make the mistake of thinking that because multiple murderers are often in the popular media that they would be easy to study," Schurman-Kauflin wrote. "Nothing could be further from the truth. These killers are difficult to work with, and the subject matter is dark."[11] Unfortunately, criminal profiling is often misunderstood by the general public. Untrained, amateur "profilers" sometimes try to help during difficult cases and make the job of catching a criminal harder for law enforcement officers and expert profilers alike.

Such was the case during the D.C. Sniper killings in 2002. There was much speculation in the media about who the killer might be and what they were going to do next. However, reading a few books and watching television shows or a movie on the subject do not make a person a profiler. "With no behavior to assess, except for accurate marksmanship, commentators ... offered all sorts of ideas," explained author and criminal justice professor Katherine Ramsland. "It soon

Though amateur profilers in the D.C. Sniper case were trying to help, their inexperience with that type of work possibly led to increased danger and slowed the police investigation. One of the snipers, John Allen Muhammad (shown here), did not fit the amateurs' profile at all.

became clear that the offender was listening to what the commentators and police were predicting, because whatever was concluded about 'him' was soon undermined."[12]

Amateur profilers stated in the news that the killer did not shoot children—but then a child was shot. After the news media printed and broadcast that the killer took weekends off from killing, the first weekend shooting took place. The unprofessional profiles provided to the media by unqualified people possibly led to even more shootings. They also led everyone, even police, down the wrong path. One profile guessed that the killer was similar to most sniper criminals in the past—white and working alone. When the case was finally solved, the sniper turned out to actually be two people: an African American man and a Jamaican teenager. Police, desperate to stop the slayings and facing pressure from the public to follow up on every lead, started looking for the wrong suspect altogether, in part because of an overload of amateur profiles from people who were not experts.

The killers, meanwhile, watched their fame increase on television, and it seemed they made a sport of the media attention. "One of them later admitted that he'd shot certain people after watching the police chief on news programs trying to anticipate their behavior,"[13] Ramsland wrote.

When the snipers were finally caught and the profiles the public had been hearing about in the news turned out to be entirely wrong, people began to have serious doubts that criminal profiling had any value at all.

Cause and Effect, Not Stereotypes and Statistics

Profiling requires a certain amount of guessing, and there is always a chance that profilers might be wrong. The difference between what expert profilers (typically FBI agents with special training and many years of experience) provided and what the public heard during the D.C. Sniper case is the important difference between deductive and inductive reasoning.

One of the most common beliefs about criminal profiling is that it creates a recipe of a type of criminal; police merely look up a profile for a standard killer (or arsonist, or carjacker) and head out to arrest someone like that. This was one of the problems in the amateur profiles created for the D.C. Sniper. Working from statistics about snipers in general to reach a conclusion about that particular criminal, amateurs used inductive reasoning to paint a picture of a single white shooter. Based on statistics, a mold was created of the type of person who would probably fit that crime.

McCrary claimed profiles based on inductive reasoning are generally "templates laid over a specific population in an attempt to predict who within that group might have an [increased] potential for committing a certain type of violence." A common problem with profiles created through inductive reasoning, he wrote, "is that they become overly inclusive and dependent on stereotyping, which can result in suspicions of the wrong people while allowing actual offenders to remain free."[14]

Expert profilers, on the other hand, look at each case individually and apply deductive reasoning. They sift through every bit of evidence investigators have, and they look for clues about the behavior of the person who left that evidence behind. "Through this intense review process, a 'behavioral' [guide] of the crime and the offender can be constructed," profiler Mary Ellen O'Toole described. "This [guide] allows a profiler to re-create what happened at the scene."[15]

Profilers try to answer two

U.S. Serial Killers Percentage by Race and Decade

Decade	Race				
	White	Black	Hispanic	Asian	Native American
1900	72.9	25.0	0.0	0.0	2.1
1910	66.7	33.3	0.0	0.0	0.0
1920	78.3	18.3	1.7	0.0	1.7
1930	69.1	30.9	0.0	0.0	0.0
1940	66.7	27.8	1.9	1.9	1.9
1950	69.4	27.8	2.8	0.0	0.0
1960	68.9	28.3	1.4	0.0	1.4
1970	60.9	33.6	4.2	0.3	1.0
1980	53.0	36.8	7.8	0.8	1.7
1990	41.4	47.1	9.0	2.0	0.5
2000	32.3	54.4	11.6	1.1	0.5
2010	30.8	59.8	8.5	0.9	0.0
TOTAL	51.7	39.8	6.7	0.9	1.0

The typical profile of a serial killer is a white male—but recent statistics reveal that is not always the case, as this information from Radford University shows.

questions: Exactly what happened, and what kind of person would do that particular thing? To answer these questions, they practice deductive reasoning, which means examining the details of one particular crime to form a theory about what one particular criminal was thinking, what kind of person would think that way, and why. From the answers to these questions, profilers come up with possible characteristics of the criminal, based on the details of that particular crime, not on statistics of similar crimes. They look at the crime as if they were the criminal, trying to understand thought processes and behavior. Deductive reasoning deals with causes and effects, not stereotypes and statistics.

Both types of reasoning might come up with the same details, such as the probable age, race, and gender of the suspect. However, profilers reason through the crime by examining the crime scene and placing themselves in the offender's shoes. They link what was done at the crime scene to why the offender would do that and what kind of life the offender probably leads. It is always a question of behavior. Profilers ask not only what and who—but also why. "A basic premise of criminal profiling is that the way a person thinks ... directs the person's behavior," Douglas wrote. "Thus, when the investigative profiler analyzes a crime scene and notes certain critical factors, he or she may be able to determine the motive and type of person who committed the crime."[16]

By the Numbers

400

number of FBI agents who were working across the country on the D.C. Sniper case

The Five Stages in the Criminal Profiling Process

When a profiler is called in to look at a new case, there are a series of general steps to follow. The first stage in creating a profile is to look at all the evidence investigators have collected. Profilers have no part in processing a crime scene. They do not dust for fingerprints or look for bloodstains on carpets; in fact, visiting the scene itself is rarely necessary. Instead, they carefully go over the evidence collected. In a murder case, they look closely at pictures of the victim that were taken at the scene. They read the autopsy report and police reports.

The Reality of TV Profilers

CBS described the characters in their television show, *Criminal Minds*, as a small, elite group of expert profilers in the FBI's Behavioral Analysis Unit who specialize in serial killings and other horrible crimes. However, the show is not very accurate, according to people who work in criminal justice, including Dr. William Huet, professor of criminal justice at Colorado Technical University. He claimed the show has viewers believing that the FBI has a huge team of profilers all analyzing a single case and making amazingly quick, accurate conclusions based on inductive reasoning. Then, they chase down the killer and arrest them. According to Huet,

> *The reason you don't see more programs dealing with actual profiling is that it's rarely exciting … In reality, it usually involves two middle-aged FBI agents, with a lot of cases under their belts, sitting around a table going over a case file in detail, jotting down the occasional note on the stereotypical yellow legal pad. There are no exciting chases, no showdowns with the bad guys, no arrests—profilers never make the arrest themselves—and of course, no dramatic sound tracks.*[1]

1. William Huet, "Uncovering the Truth: The Reality of Criminal Profiling," Colorado Technical University, October 11, 2012. www.coloradotech.edu/resources/blogs/october-2012/criminal-profiling.

The cast of Criminal Minds, *shown here, is often shown solving one case. In reality, the group of profilers is smaller and generally involves only two people.*

They note every detail of the crime, down to what the weather was like that day. There is only one detail a profiler does not want: any information on possible suspects. This is because they want their profile to be constructed only using information from the crime; if they had a suspect's information, they might unconsciously try to match their work to fit the suspect, instead of the other way around.

The second stage in the profiling process is to classify the crime. In a murder case, the profiler looks at the number of victims and what the killer's thought process might have been. Profilers decide, based on the evidence, whether the killer knew the victim or victims and if so, how well. They also ask whether the criminal truly meant to kill anyone or whether it was an accident. The next stage is to reconstruct the crime itself, including the murderer's behaviors and motivations and the profile of the victim. During the fourth stage, based on the information collected, they create a profile of the killer. As profilers work, they are constantly referencing the original evidence collected in the case. If they come up with something that does not seem to add up correctly, they will immediately address it before they finish the profile.

At the final stage, the process is complete and the profiler hands it over to the team that is investigating the case. A finished profile may change if new evidence is discovered. A profiler always tries to make sure that everything in the profile matches all the available clues the killer left behind, and that sometimes means taking new evidence into account as the case develops.

Stranger Crimes

If there are known suspects in a crime, police compare them to the profile. Often, however, the kinds of crimes for which criminal profiles are requested are the crimes in which investigators have few or no leads. Typically, they are also crimes that desperately need to be solved quickly. When an expert profiler from the FBI is called to the case, it generally means a violent and dangerous serial criminal is on the loose. "The investigation of serial violent and sexual crime is complex and difficult," profiling expert D. Kim Rossmo wrote. "Most murders are solved because they involve intimates [someone the victim knows], and the search for the offender begins with the victim's family, friends, and acquaintances."[17] There is no such obvious relationship, however, in the kinds of crimes in which most profilers specialize. These are often called "stranger crimes," or crimes with no clear motive or link between the criminal and the victim.

One crime like this is frightening enough, but when a string of seemingly connected crimes begins to take place, police quickly become desperate. The longer the criminal remains free, the more victims there will potentially be. This is when the phone at the FBI starts to ring, and a profiler gets on the next plane to meet with the investigators who are working on the crime.

Chapter Two
Crime Scene Analysis

Profilers are not commonly at the scene of the crime, but the evidence left there is the heart of their investigation. While the profiler will examine the physical evidence collected during an investigation, such as clothing fibers caught on a branch, bullet casings, and blood samples, there are things a profiler is looking at in a crime scene that other investigators do not see.

Profilers try to find clues at the crime scene that might be a link to certain types of criminal behavior. Where the crime was committed, the cause of death, the position of the victim's body, and the type and location of the wounds are all elements that are critically important to a profiler and could be easily ignored by less experienced investigators.

Assessment of the Scene

Most profiles are made up of a professional analysis of a crime paired with the profiler's expert opinion about what kind of person would do such a thing. "I use a formula," explained John E. Douglas. "'How plus Why equals Who.' If we can answer the hows and whys in a crime, we generally can come up with the solution."[18]

Profilers are not generally part of the crime scene investigation itself. They are typically called in after the physical evidence at the crime scene has already been collected. This is because few local police forces have criminal profilers on staff. Instead, these professionals are generally based at the FBI headquarters in Virginia or at field offices around the country. Profilers want an objective view of the crime. They look at all the evidence and draw their own, independent conclusions. A suggestion made by someone else could possibly influence their thinking about what really took place. When profilers analyze a crime scene, they generally do much of the work on paper, examining all the evidence, photographs, and police reports—they do not frequently interview the police officers who collected the evidence.

Profilers start with the location that the crime took place. This is sometimes a challenge, because serial crimes almost always take place in multiple locations. The police commonly know only one location at first—where the body was found. However, this may not have been where the person was killed. It may not have been where the killer first contacted the victim, either. Therefore, a complete crime scene can involve many different places, such as a department store parking lot where the victim was taken, the basement where the victim was killed, the river where the victim's body was dumped, and the vehicle that carried the victim's body in between. "The specific location set for a given crime," D. Kim Rossmo wrote, "implies something about the offender, how he or she searches for victims and the associated level of organization and mobility. Generally, the greater the organization and mobility of the offender, the greater the potential complexity (i.e., the more separate locations) of the crime location set."[19] Deciding on the scene of a crime is even more complicated when a killer purposely tries to deceive police by staging the crime scene. Some killers try to fool police into thinking the murder might actually have taken place in one location, when it was really done somewhere else.

Fortunately, expert profilers can look at clues and put together what really happened. They might recognize signs, for example, that the victim was killed somewhere other than where the body was found or where the murderer tried to make police think the killing happened. Although it complicates the crime, staging also tells profilers a lot about the killer. From the way the body and the final crime scene look, a profiler can often tell police not only the type of place that was likely the scene of the murder, but in what kind of place the killer probably found his victim—for example, a crowded parking lot or a deserted hiking trail. A profiler can figure all this out just by the way a killer organizes the scene.

By the Numbers

65

percentage of victims of serial killers who were lured in by the killer's premeditated plan

An Unorganized, Brutal Attack

Profiling is based largely on the question of how well the killer plans out their actions. There are killers who act on impulse, exploding into violence with little or no plan for what they will do after, or even during, the event. There are also killers who carefully plan every detail of the crime in advance, down to the steps they will take to avoid being caught. The first type of killer works very differently than the second, and the scene of the crime reflects this.

In January 1978, a brutal killer was terrorizing Sacramento, California. He broke into two different homes during a single week and killed five people, badly mutilating the bodies. The sheriff of Sacramento County told newspapers that the crimes were the most grotesque he had encountered in three decades of police work. The killer came to be known as the Vampire of Sacramento because of evidence at the scenes that indicated he drank the blood of his victims.

Fortunately, two different profilers gave police detailed—and extremely accurate—profiles of the killer's personality and where they would find him. The profilers' first clues came from looking at the crime scenes. They were classic disorganized crime scenes. In a disorganized crime scene, there is evidence that the crime was committed suddenly, with little or no planning. The actual murder took place quickly and violently. The victim in a disorganized crime scene was clearly taken by surprise. A disorganized murderer generally silences the victim quickly, because the plan is not well thought out and he fears his victim might fight back or make enough noise to draw attention to the scene. Disorganized crime scenes are often signs of a killer who has poor intelligence and most likely suffers from a mental illness.

Russell Vorpagel, one of the FBI profilers who worked on the Vampire of Sacramento slayings, concluded that the killer's mental illness caused him to shoot the victims before mutilating their bodies. "This type of crime—an unorganized, brutal ... attack, with no logical motive—was done by a seriously mentally disturbed person."[20] The profilers' assessments of the Sacramento Vampire's crime scenes led them to other conclusions, as well. The killer was probably white, because his victims were white and murderers tend to kill people who are of their own race. Based on similarities with other crime scenes they had analyzed in the past, the profilers also suspected that the killer probably lived alone in a filthy home. Also, because disorganized killers commonly act on impulse and live within walking distance of their crimes, the profilers predicted the Vampire of Sacramento's home would be within 1 mile (1.6 km) of both crime scenes.

These and other details in the profiles helped police track down the killer. Once they knew they would be looking for a certain type of man who lived within a mile of the murders,

When police arrested Richard Chase at his home, evidence was found linking him to all the Sacramento murders. He became infamous and was even added to a serial killer calendar—a page of which is shown here.

the search became much easier. The profile undoubtedly assisted in saving time for the police. They had the exact area the killer would likely be in, which massively cut down on the amount of time they had to spend searching. The race was on, because the profilers in the case also predicted the killer would strike again soon if he was not caught. The Vampire of Sacramento, Richard Trenton Chase, was captured five days after his first murders and one day after the murders at the second crime scene. He had a history of mental illness, as the profiles had predicted. He eventually received the death penalty for his horrible crimes.

Profilers recognize disorganized crime scenes like those of the Vampire of Sacramento in many ways. Not only is there evidence that the victim was suddenly and violently attacked, often from behind, but disorganized crime scenes also tend to be messy. They commonly involve only one location. The killer murders his victims where he finds them and leaves the bodies at the scene. There is a lot of physical evidence to be collected at a disorganized scene, including fingerprints and footprints. The killer acts impulsively, taking little or no time to cover their trail or hide what they have done. The murder weapon is frequently left behind at a disorganized crime scene, too. In many cases, the weapon even comes from the scene itself, such as a knife taken from the victim's kitchen.

With so many leads and so much evidence, disorganized crimes are easy to solve, relative to other kinds of killings. "Disorganized offenders are just that: disorganized," wrote one expert. "Often, the more disorganized a crime scene, the more likely the individual suffers from psychosis. It follows that disorganized killers are more often one-time killers than serial offenders because they are more easily caught."[21] However, disorganized killers can and do avoid getting caught. Many modern profilers believe that the infamous 19th century London slayer Jack the Ripper was a disorganized criminal, and he was never caught.

Unfortunately, violent murderers are not always caught quickly, even when the best profilers are at work on the case. Some killing sprees last decades. Generally, this type of killer leaves behind a crime scene that shows evidence of planning down to the tiniest details, sometimes even taunting police for their inability to catch the killer. Profilers characterize these kinds of crime scenes as organized, and when they look at the evidence from one, they know they are probably facing a difficult case.

Order and Chaos

Scenes of murders and other violent crimes may be organized, showing that the crime was planned, or disorganized, showing that the offender acted on impulse. Here are some of the ways profilers tell them apart:

Organized Scene:

- The location was carefully chosen and out of sight.
- The victim was restrained.
- The body was hidden from view or moved somewhere else.
- The murder weapon and other physical evidence was removed from the scene.
- The offender left no physical evidence or tried to cover it up.
- Damage to the body was done before death.

Disorganized Scene:

- The victim was killed swiftly, not restrained.
- The body was left in plain sight, generally right at the murder scene.
- The murder weapon was a weapon of convenience, something found at the scene during the attack.
- The offender left physical evidence behind.
- Damage to the body was done after death.

Most crime scenes are mixed—partly organized, partly disorganized. Nonetheless, these characteristics are still important behavioral clues that can point profilers in a new direction.

Planned and Premeditated

In profiling an organized killer, a profiler notices several key factors at the scene of the murder, including planning and premeditation. There is evidence that the killer knew what they were going to do for quite a while before they did it and that once it was done, they took steps to hide the crime, their involvement in the crime, or both. In a case of organized murder, the killer may select a secluded or isolated area in which to commit the murder. Alternatively, the victim may be transported to another location other than where they were killed. Robert K. Ressler and Ann W. Burgess made an example of a case in which the bodies of several female victims were found in various rivers, weighed down with car parts that had been tied to their bodies. "There were indications that they had been kept for several days before being

WANTED

SAN FRANCISCO POLICE DEPARTMENT

NO. 90-69 WANTED FOR MURDER OCTOBER 18, 1969

ORIGINAL DRAWING

AMENDED DRAWING

Supplementing our Bulletin 87-69 of October 13, 1969. Additional information has developed the above amended drawing of murder suspect known as "ZODIAC".

WMA, 35-45 Years, approximately 5'8", Heavy Build, Short Brown Hair, possibly with Red Tint, Wears Glasses. Armed with 9 MM Automatic.

Available for comparison: Slugs, Casings, Latents, Handwriting.

ANY INFORMATION:
Inspectors Armstrong & Toschi
Homicide Detail
CASE NO. 696314

THOMAS J. CAHILL
CHIFF OF POLICE

The Zodiac Killer, one of America's most famous serial murderers, was both intelligent and deadly, carrying out a series of organized murders and attempted murders. He left behind a series of deliberate clues, trying to taunt police officers into catching him. He was never identified.

Types of Serial Killers

Some criminologists have reclassified the organized and disorganized characteristics of serial killers into four different categories:

Visionary: Frequently psychotic and motivated by a force compelling them to destroy a person or group of people, visionary killers target victims who are random strangers within close proximity to their home; their murders are disorganized.

Mission oriented: Compelled to kill a certain group of people but motivated by personal beliefs and a sense of righteousness, mission oriented murderers are planned and organized.

Pleasure seeking: This type of murderer kills for pleasure and excitement and is motivated by the victim's terror. They are typically are a mixture of organized and disorganized.

Power or control: Motivated by having complete control over the victim's life and death, killers interested in power or control look for specific—typically vulnerable—victims. Their murders are organized.

thrown into the river. The murderer would have needed a car to transport them from where they were last seen alive to where their bodies were discovered."[22]

Crime scenes with multiple locations are considered organized. Multiple locations suggest that the killer took steps to cover their tracks—meaning a lot of thought went into the crime. The scenes are not impulsive and frenzied, like disorganized crimes. The primary signs of organized crime scenes, from a profiler's point of view, are evidence of planning and premeditation. Organized killers do not always try to hide evidence and avoid detection. Some of the most notorious serial murderers, in fact, do just the opposite, leaving behind deliberate clues and matching wits with the law enforcement officers who are trying to catch them.

Both kinds of offenders leave clues for the detectives on the case. These are two of the most important factors to take into account when investigating most crimes, particularly of serial crimes. The first is modus operandi. The second—often much more sinister—is a signature.

Modus Operandi

Modus operandi, or m.o. for short, is a Latin term that translates to "method of operating." A criminal's m.o. is what they do to carry out a crime to its completion. An m.o.—unique to each serial criminal—has different steps, each one aimed at helping the criminal to do three things: protect their identity, carry out the crime, and escape from the scene. In a robbery, a burglar's m.o. might include wearing gloves to avoid leaving fingerprints behind, deactivating an alarm system so it does not go off, and jumping into a stolen car to escape from the scene. The m.o. of serial rapists and murderers typically includes more disturbing habits. Offenders might wear masks or disguises to protect their identity from their victims. They might prevent their victims from calling for help by gagging them or by luring them to a secluded place. They might make their escape by tying up their victims—or killing them—so they cannot get away and call the police.

An m.o. is important to solving cases, particularly serial crimes, because it can help police determine if the same person committed different crimes. Knowing the m.o. of criminals who have been caught can also help police find new suspects in unsolved cases or eliminate other convicted suspects who clearly have a different m.o. "It is reasonable to say that all criminals have an MO, but that MO is not necessarily all that distinctive," wrote Brent E. Turvey, an expert in criminal profiling. "Even when the MO in otherwise unconnected cases is precisely the same, a reasonable level of certainty has not been reached with respect to the absolute identity of the offender."[23] In other words, explained Turvey, similar methods of operating might only mean that two or more criminals have found that a certain way of committing a crime keeps them from getting caught. In fact, he wrote, criminals who spend time in prison often network with other convicts and learn even more about how to avoid getting caught when they are released from prison.

Accordingly, an m.o. is only one of the things a criminal profiler considers in deciding what kind of person committed a certain crime. For profilers, the m.o. is most useful when it reveals something specific about the criminal, something that makes them stand out from the rest. For example, an m.o. may point to a certain skill or line of work in which the criminal may have experience. Tying up victims using a certain kind of knot could be the mark of an outdoorsman, a professional sailor, or a fisherman. Evidence that a criminal planned a perfect escape route from the building

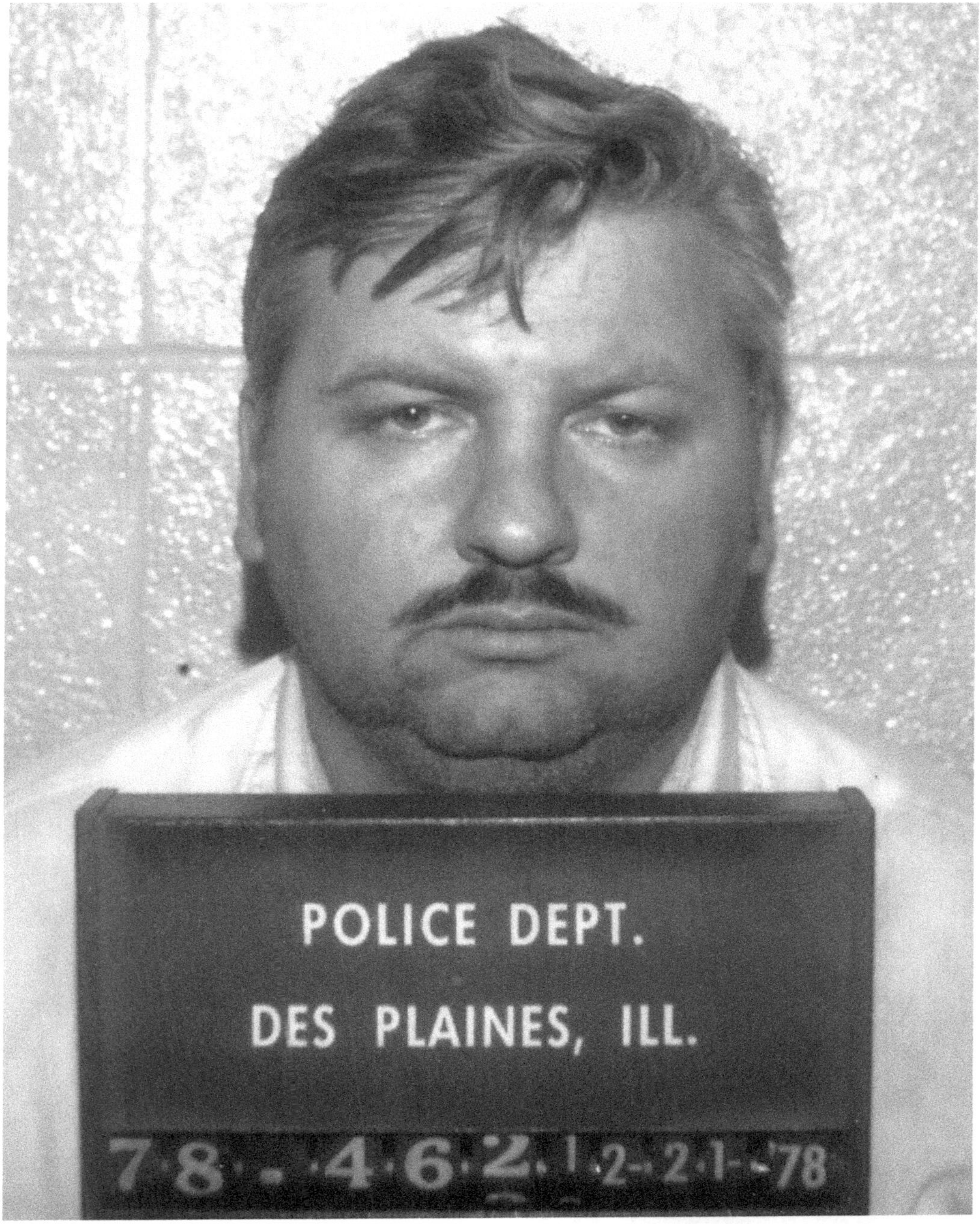

In the 1970s, John Wayne Gacy raped and murdered 33 young men and hid the remains of 29 of the victims in a crawlspace under his house. His m.o. was to strangle most of them with a rope.

of a crime scene could help a profiler determine that police should look for a person who knows that building very well, possibly because they live or work there.

A criminal's m.o. can also change, and it often does. If a crime goes badly for them, they may learn from their mistakes and do things a bit differently the next time. It could also go the other way. A serial killer who suffers from a mental illness may begin to kill more often, and they might start to get sloppy. Their m.o. might actually weaken over time. Profilers often look for this kind of change in the cases they examine. The changes in m.o. from one serial crime to the next can tell them a great deal about the kind of person committing the crimes. Killers who get craftier are typically organized, and those who get messier are generally disorganized. However, changing an m.o. can also make it hard to link cases committed by the same person. That is why criminal profilers also depend on another clue, one that does not change so much between crimes—a criminal's signature.

By the Numbers

9.7

percent of increase of violent crimes in U.S. cities between 2015 and 2016

Signatures

An m.o. is typically developed for efficiency. A burglar, for example, wants to get the crime over with and get away from the scene as soon as possible. Their motivation is cash or valuables. Serial killers and rapists, on the other hand, are motivated by different things. Many commit their crimes for the very sake of committing them. Therefore, they do certain things during their crimes that make the act more meaningful to them. These things are called signatures. They are not done for the purpose of carrying out the crime, but for satisfying certain psychological or emotional needs. In fact, signatures may even hinder the crime, sometimes making it more likely that the victim will escape or that someone will catch the criminal in the act.

Profilers typically find signatures very useful in creating an accurate picture of a criminal. However, "the manifestation of modus operandi behaviors and signature behaviors are not always readily apparent to even the most competent criminal profilers," Turvey wrote. Nonetheless, in the right circumstances, "a specific pattern of signature behaviors and the needs that they represent can be used to distinguish between crime scenes and potentially between offenders."[24]

Douglas gave the following example: "Take the case of a bank robber in Texas who made all of his captives undress ... and took photographs of them. That's his signature. It was not necessary or helpful to the commission of the bank robbery. In fact, it kept him there longer and therefore placed him in greater jeopardy of being caught." Douglas compared this signature with that of a bank robber in Grand Rapids, Michigan, who also made everyone in the bank undress. The difference, Douglas explained, was that the robber in Michigan "did it so the witnesses would be so preoccupied and embarrassed that they wouldn't be looking at him and so couldn't make a positive ID later on. This was a means toward successfully robbing the bank. This was MO."[25]

Separating an m.o. from a signature and linking these two elements in related crime scenes is one of a profiler's most important challenges. Failing to make these connections can lead to something profilers call linkage blindness, or the inability to draw similarities that connect one case to another and prove a serial offender is at work. Profilers must have excellent memories for such details. Because many profilers work for the FBI, they work all over the United States, often over several decades. Some serial killers also commit their crimes in different locations around the country and sometimes even over the course of several decades. The basic signature of a serial criminal rarely changes. Remembering a signature and unique m.o. from one unsolved case could prove useful for the profiler when a strangely similar set of characteristics is found at the scene of another crime. Serial criminals, after all, are often mobile. As profilers evaluate crime scenes in different cities, they sometimes must compare the details to crimes in other cities.

Profiling the Location

As the world becomes increasingly mobile, so do some serial criminals. One factor profilers must consider when they examine details of a crime scene is the geography of the area where the crime occurred. Geographic profiling is based on the idea that examining the locations and times at which a series of crimes took place can tell profilers a great deal about where the offender is likely to live and where and when they might strike again. Research has indicated "a high level of consistency in the geographic modus operandi of serial offenders, as most repeatedly employ

A Calling Card

Investigators on the trail of 1940s serial killer William Heirens found the words "For heaven's sake catch me before I kill more. I cannot control myself"[1] scribbled in lipstick on the wall of one of the murder scenes. Heirens did not leave a lipstick note behind at all three of his brutal murders; just the same, this message was an important signature—a clue about his state of mind. Equally telling was the fact that he urinated and defecated at the scenes of his crimes. Such behaviors, unnecessary to carrying out the crime, are a profiler's most useful type of evidence. However, few offenders actually take the time to "sign" their crimes in such a personality-revealing way.

Albert DeSalvo, the Boston Strangler of the 1960s, tied a bow under the chin of his victims, using socks or other garments, to let the police know he had struck again. Not all offenders have such obvious signatures. If a criminal does have a signature, it may never be obvious unless they are caught and later admit to it.

1. Quoted in Douglas Martin, "William Heirens, the 'Lipstick Killer,' Dies at 83," *New York Times*, March 7, 2012. www.nytimes.com/2012/03/07/us/william-heirens-the-lipstick-killer-dies-at-83.html.

William Heirens was called the Lipstick Killer after leaving this note in lipstick on the wall of one of his murder scenes.

the same crime location set," Rossmo wrote. "This implies that the concept of crime location set could be used as an assessment characteristic for the linking of serial offenses."[26]

Considering similar locations, however, does not always mean that crimes take place in the same town, or even the same state. In fact, the more organized an offender is, the more likely they may be to change cities and throw investigators off their trail. Profilers hoping to track such a criminal across multiple states, or even countries, must look carefully at the setting of the crimes. Killers may change cities, but their crimes will often still take place in the same general locations—bodies may always be found along the side of a major highway, for example, or in a motel room. The ability to draw connections between crimes, whether they take place across the street from one another or across the country, is one of the important talents of a profiler.

Once the crime scene has been carefully analyzed for clues and the profiler has determined what was done and how, there are still more questions to answer. Next, the profiler must learn about who was killed and determine why the killer chose this person.

Chapter Three
The Victim's Story

Historically, the victims of serial criminal offenders have been given very little attention in the criminal profiling process. The BAU has been working hard to change that. The unit collects information about the victim's physical characteristics, their daily activities, medical and marital histories, education, occupation, and criminal history. Knowing as much as possible about the victim makes it easier for law enforcement to identify a pool of suspects. Victims of violent crimes are rarely left alive to tell their stories. It is the job of the criminal profiler to tell their stories for them.

Victims and Offenders

The study of crime victims, called victimology, is considered one of the most important steps in solving crimes. In violent crimes, the victim is the most important piece of evidence investigators have. The victim is the solid proof that a crime was committed. Whether the victim survived the encounter or not, the offender and the victim spent time together. Their paths crossed somehow. How these people—victim and criminal—ended up in the same place at the same time is an important answer profilers seek when they study any violent crime.

In many cases of rape or murder, the offender and the victim know each other before the incident. When making a list of suspects, investigators look first at family, friends, coworkers, and other people who were close to the victim. "A thorough understanding of the victim," explained criminal justice experts Mike King and Greg Cooper, "can often lead the investigation toward a probable suspect rather than … to an endless pool of less likely possible candidates."[27] By examining who the victim was, profilers can create accurate lists of potential suspects while eliminating leads that would waste their time.

Method by Which Victim Was Killed		
Method of Death	**Number**	**Percent**
shot	4,259	42.96%
strangled	2,156	21.71%
stabbed	1,471	14.84%
bludgeoned	910	9.18%
poisoned	714	7.20%
axed	145	1.46%
drowned	94	0.95%
burned	63	0.64%
smothered	61	0.62%
run over	19	0.19%
drug overdose	16	0.16%
neglect and abuse	10	0.10%
TOTAL	9,915	

Using data collected by Radford University from 1920 to 2015, this chart shows how serial killers committed their crimes.

According to traditional criminal investigation logic, victimology generally leads to a motive, which in turn leads to suspects and eventually, the offender. Many murder investigations are solved because a victim's circumstances show an obvious motive. A crime of fury or passion may point to an angry spouse or ex-significant other. A murder victim who recently took out a large life insurance policy commonly leads police to look first at the person who would collect all that money.

Many of the cases that profilers take on, however, are the ones with no clear motive and no easy answers. Often, they are the cases with evidence, based on modus operandi and signature, that a serial criminal is at work. "While it is not completely accurate to say that these crimes are motiveless," Douglas wrote, "the motive may all too often be one understood only by the perpetrator."[28] Serial crimes are not isolated offenses for revenge or money. A serial offender tries to hunt people. A criminal profiler can use victimology to determine who falls into the hunter's sights, why, and what this says about the hunter. What makes some serial criminals hard to catch—and especially terrifying—is that they seem to find victims at random. Police face a difficult challenge in the race to find out how the offender works and who might be targeted next.

An investigator's job might be easier if a killer was targeting employees of a particular department store every Saturday evening. Aside from just staking out the parking lot on Saturday nights, it would be easy to conclude that the killer must be someone who knows the employees of the store because they spend a lot of time there. The initial list of suspects would rapidly shrink down to include the store's employees and regular customers—a manageable list for investigators. Far more difficult to catch is the serial offender whose victims show no such obvious relationship to one another. In these cases, profilers must make educated guesses about why the offender chose these particular victims.

By the Numbers

15

number of serial killers who murdered three or more people in the United States in 2015

Psychological Detective Work

Profilers in murder cases ask questions about the killer's behavior during four crime phases:

Antecedent: What was the killer's plan? Why did the killer commit the act on a particular day?

Method and manner: What type of victim was chosen? How was the murder carried out—was it a stabbing, a shooting, or something else?

Body disposal: Was the murder committed at the scene, or was the victim killed elsewhere and placed there?

Postoffensive behavior: Is the killer contacting the police or the media to get attention?

High-Risk Victims

People who rarely venture into dangerous situations are considered by profilers to have a low risk of becoming victims of violent crime. A stay-at-home mother who had young children, lived in a safe neighborhood in a home with an alarm system, and rarely went out alone after dark would be considered a low-risk victim, because nothing in her life would ordinarily put her in danger.

A victim classified as medium risk would have had a slightly more dangerous lifestyle. This might be someone who worked the evening shift at a bar or a convenience store, lived alone in an apartment in a dangerous part of town, or preferred to walk to the store for groceries after work late at night.

High-risk victims are people whose lifestyle frequently would have put them in harm's way. They may have had a drug habit and had spent a lot of time with drug dealers or other criminals. Sex workers, because of their working hours and locations, are always at high risk for crime. However, a college student with no car and no money could also be at a high risk if they accept a ride from a stranger to make it home for Thanksgiving.

Profilers frequently try to determine the risk level of a particular

Gary Ridgway, the Green River Killer, pled guilty to murdering 48 women between 1982 and 2001. He said he chose sex workers as victims because they would not be reported missing to the police right away.

victim. It has nothing to do with passing judgment on a victim and everything to do with deciding what kind of criminal is at work and how the offender is selecting their prey. The more investigators can learn about a victim, the greater chance they will have at also learning some valuable information about their attacker. Cases that involve low-risk victims are commonly easier to profile because these victims are more likely to have been targeted for crime by someone they knew or by someone they had met before. On the other hand, high-risk victims could be targeted by a wide variety of people simply because of their lifestyle or a certain choice they made, such as accepting a ride from strangers.

Finding Patterns in the Details

There have been countless cases in which the criminal was apprehended due to the diligence, hard work, and perception of a criminal profiler. One of the keys to the investigation of a serial offender is to look for the smallest details connecting the crimes. For example, if someone was breaking into houses and murdering single women, profilers may first look at the geographic location of the crime scenes. They could take notes on how close together they are or determine that the killer is striking only homes within a certain radius—which would mean that the criminal likely lives nearby. Additionally, the profiler may notice that all the victims are single women of a particular age, which could teach them a lot about the kind of person the offender is targeting. Moreover, if the killer attacks only single women, the profiler will ask how they knew the victims were all single. This could lead them to the documents about bank loans used to purchase the victim's homes. Maybe the killer is a bank loan officer, who is targeting their clients.

In this example, if investigators found that all the victims used the same bank to purchase their homes, their suspect list will shorten considerably to include only employees working at that bank. This part of victimology—finding out how victims can be related and connected—can often be one of the strongest tools in a profiler's arsenal. However, things are rarely as easy as connecting bank loans to loan officers. There could seemingly be no connections between victims, which dramatically slows down an investigation. Still, profilers will ask many questions about victims because, in serial crimes, the type of person who catches a criminal's attention can be a huge clue to the type of offender the criminal is. Profilers want to know all they can about victims in a case, because patterns in the way the victims look, where they live, or where they work might be clues about whom the offender will go after the next time.

In murder cases, profilers also want to know where the victims were last seen alive, where the bodies were found, and whether either location is where the murders actually took place. "It is necessary to determine what the last known location of the victim was," explained one expert. "Did the victim end up in that particular location because the predator chose it, or is it a place where the victim visited or stayed in regular circumstances?"[29] These details are clues not only to a killer's strategy for finding victims but also to the type of offender the killer is: organized or disorganized.

Circumstance and Trickery

In the 19th century, Jack the Ripper's victims were high-risk women: sex workers. He murdered them on the streets of London where he found them and made little or no effort to move or hide their bodies when he was done. Modern profilers would have seen some classic signs of a disorganized killer in Jack the Ripper. Based on the state of his victims, he killed with sudden violence, mutilated

Occupation: Forensic Psychologist

Job Description:
A forensic psychologist studies and analyzes criminals and crime scenes to assist in developing a criminal profile. They evaluate suspects to determine their degree of sanity at the time of the crime and whether they are fit to stand trial. Many forensic psychologists are asked to give expert testimony in criminal trials.

Education:
Forensic psychologists are required to have a master's or doctorate degree in psychology, plus additional education in the specialized subfield of forensic psychology.

Qualifications:
Forensic psychologists must hold a license to practice psychology in their state and must pass a state certification exam to ensure they meet certain standards. Experience in the related field of criminal justice is a bonus. Forensic psychologists can specialize in many different areas; they may work for prisons, psychiatric hospitals, law enforcement agencies, juvenile detention centers, or private consulting firms. Excellent people skills and communication skills are essential in this job.

Salary:
The median annual salary for a forensic psychologist in 2016 was $70,700.

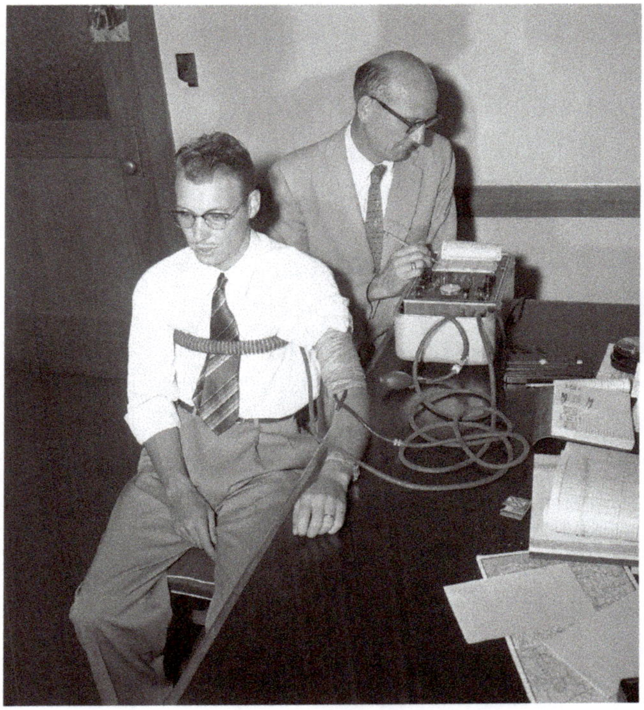

Lie detector tests can be useful to any criminal investigation, but especially in cases of serial murder. Forensic psychologists sometimes analyze the results of a suspect's tests to get a better perspective on their mindset.

the bodies of his victims after they were dead, and left their bodies in plain view at the death scene—all typical signs of a killer with a disorganized personality.

A very different scene is one in which the victim is discovered in a place far from where they were last seen, a place where that person would not normally have spent time. These details point to a more organized offender who planned the abduction. When a victim's body is found in an unexpected place—for example, in a forest in the middle of winter wearing nothing but a thin shirt—it suggests that the killer found the victim somewhere other than where they eventually left the body. This kind of killer does not ambush their victims right where they live or work; instead, they may try to trick their targets into going somewhere with them. Profilers might be looking for a much more cunning killer, one whose victims will not be limited to high-risk people but will also include anyone they are able to trick.

Ted Bundy, who murdered at least 30 people in the 1970s, was a con artist like this. A particularly organized offender who left almost no physical evidence behind on his deadly trail across several states, Bundy captured most of his victims by luring them close with an act that he was injured on crutches or with his arm in a sling and needed help getting items to his car. He then turned on them violently when they got near. Profilers carefully study the victims of a killer such as Bundy, trying to determine just what these people would have been likely to believe and how probable it is that they would, for instance, willingly get into a killer's car.

Only then does a profiler get an idea what law enforcement officers are up against and just how organized, persuasive, and clever the serial criminal is. "The degree of organization or disorganization can provide tremendous insights into the level of sophistication of the offender," O'Toole explained, "including the approach used in accessing the victim, the style of attack, the relationship of the victim to the offender, and the type of interaction that likely took place at the scene between the offender and the victim."[30]

Wrong Place, Wrong Time?

Perhaps the most frightening thing about serial criminals is that in almost all cases, there will be more victims unless the criminal is caught and stopped. Whether these new victims will be strangers to the criminal or people that they have a reason to know is an important detail.

Profile of a Female Killer

In many cases of serial murder, the victims that profilers study are women who have been killed by a man. In 1989 and 1990, however, several male murder victims turned up unclothed on the side of a road, and the profile pointed to a serial killer few investigators had seen before or since: a female murderer who targeted men.

The killer, Aileen Wuornos, murdered at least seven men before she was captured. Unlike most sexually-motivated serial killers, who are males victimizing women, she was a rare example of a woman who victimized men. After shooting her victims, she generally removed their clothing and left them in wooded areas. She was arrested in 1991 and executed in 2002. Wuornos was portrayed by actress Charlize Theron in the 2003 film *Monster* and by Lily Rabe in the 2015 season of *American Horror Story*.

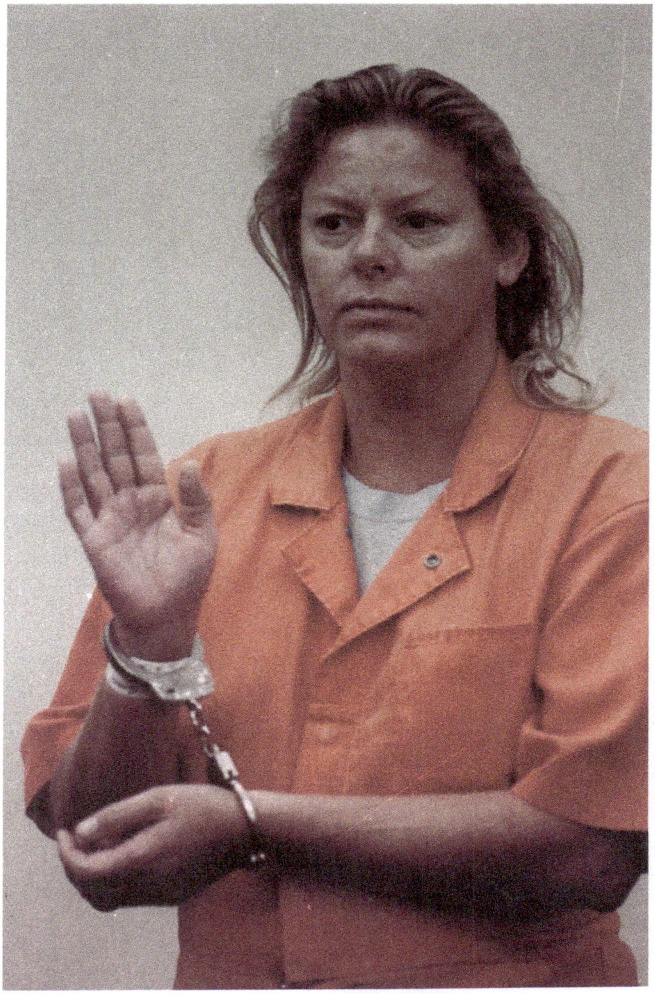

Aileen Wuornos was sexually abused as a child and was thrown out of her home as a teenager. She made a living as a sex worker and killed the men she picked up on Florida's highways.

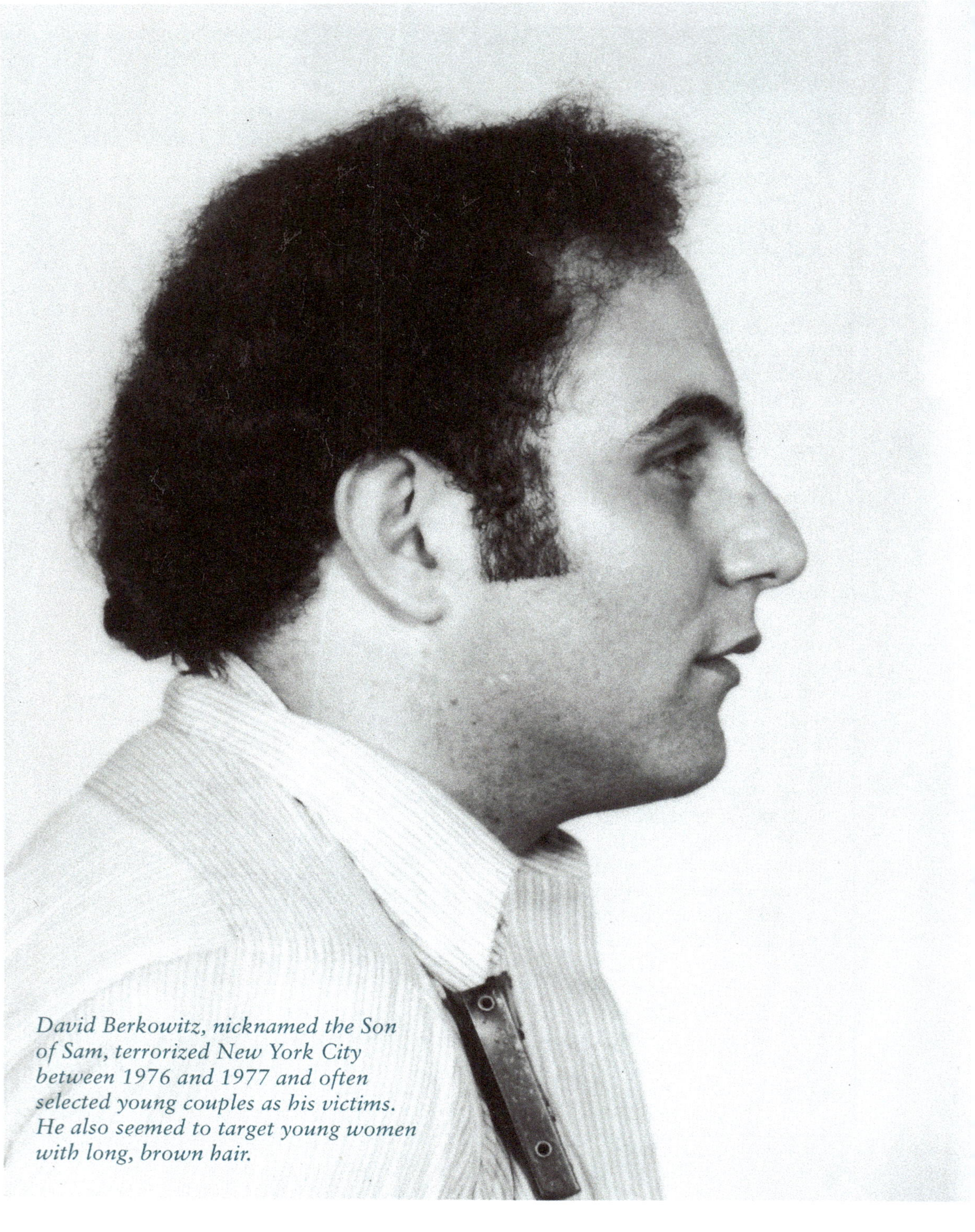

David Berkowitz, nicknamed the Son of Sam, terrorized New York City between 1976 and 1977 and often selected young couples as his victims. He also seemed to target young women with long, brown hair.

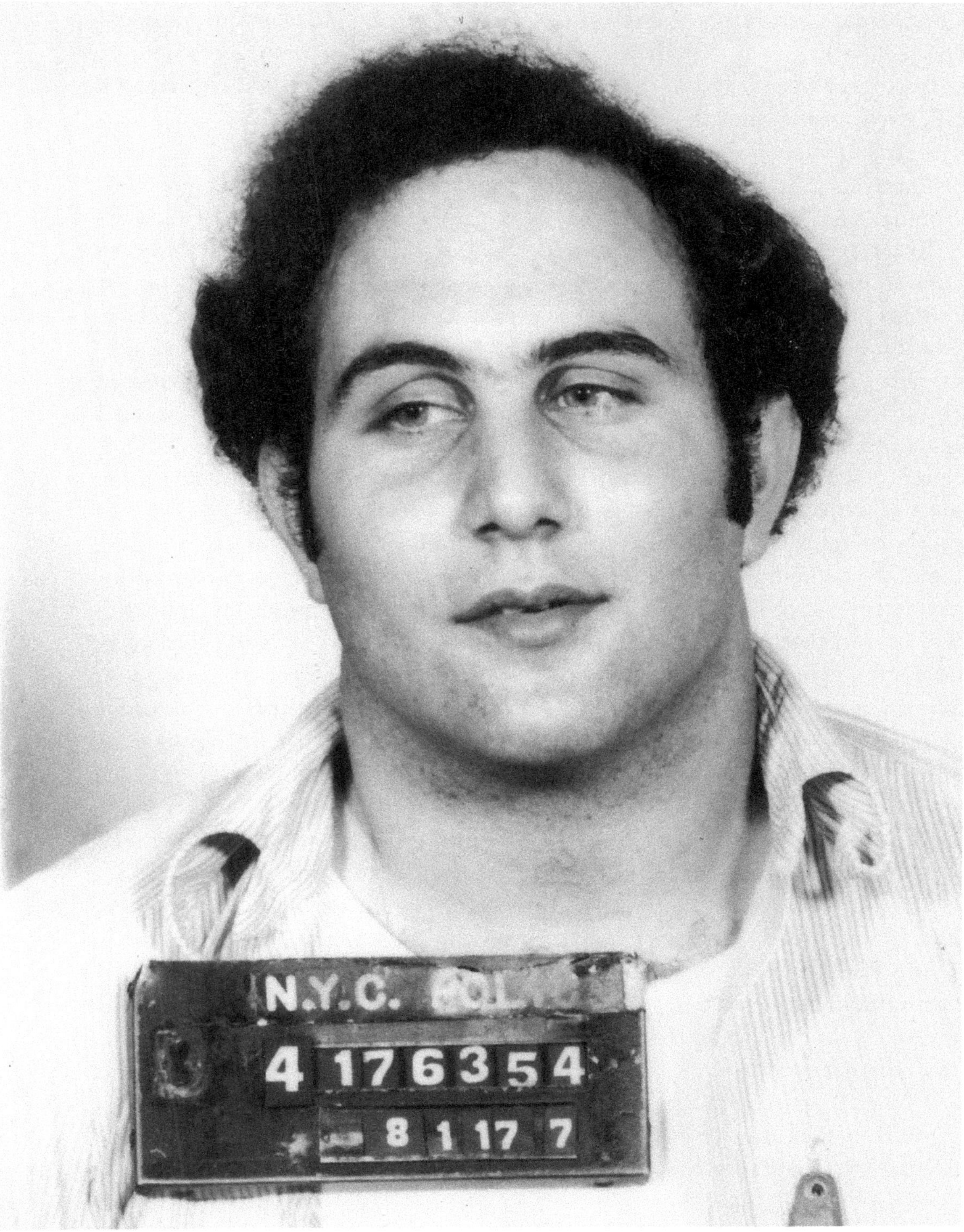
N.Y.C. POL
4 176354
8 1 17 7

Knowledge of the relationship between a killer and their victims helps determine the method the killer will use to find their next victim, and it also points to the kind of fantasies that are going on in the criminal's head.

To an experienced profiler with a good understanding of criminal psychology, whether an offender seeks out total strangers or acquaintances will point to important details about the offender. Most serial killers and rapists live in an elaborate fantasy world. When the appearance or attitude of the other person in those fantasies is important to them, they commonly spend time targeting the exact kind of victim who will best fit the role. Another offender might have fantasies about situations, not about people. For this criminal, how and where they find their victims is generally more important to the fantasy than the victims themselves.

"A prior relationship between the victim and the offender therefore need not, and typically does not, exist," wrote Richard N. Kocsis, an expert criminologist. "What is important is the role that the victim represents in the offender's fantasy."[31]

Victims of the same offender will often have similarities in appearance, personality, or other characteristics, and from this, profilers may be able to determine the kind of victims at risk of being the offender's next target.

For some offenders, a victim's characteristics, or even gender, are not the important feature of the fantasy. Instead, an offender may be obsessed with situations. They may be motivated by the thrill of the chase and the excitement of almost getting caught in the act. This kind of offender may purposefully target low-risk victims.

O'Toole wrote that understanding the risk level of both the victim and the offender is important to profiling a case: "Two possible explanations [of risk taking] are that 1) the offender targeted that particular victim, or 2) this offender needed an element of high risk/high thrill in the crime to be emotionally or psychologically satisfied. Either conclusion reached by the profiler can be extremely helpful to investigators."[32] Whether a profiler determines that a victim was targeted or was simply at the wrong place at the wrong time, getting to know the victims of a case can lead to important predictions about the offender—details that, when shared with the public, might help potential victims protect themselves.

By the Numbers

21

percent of serial killers who have previously had definite or suspected head injuries

Clues to the Connection

Carefully investigating the victims of violent crimes not only allows a profiler to determine a great deal about the perpetrator, but it can also help them determine whether the crimes were committed by a serial offender. When Albert DeSalvo, nicknamed the Boston Strangler, raped and strangled more than a dozen women to death in their Massachusetts homes in the 1960s, he left a calling card behind: pantyhose or another piece of clothing tied in a bow under his victim's chin. Police quickly knew they had a serial killer to catch.

Not all criminals work in such obvious ways. Carefully examining the background of murder victims is the only way to reveal hidden clues that link victims no one thought were related, thus exposing the work of a sneakier serial killer. Such was the case among the victims of a 1950s serial rapist and killer named Harvey Glatman. Other than the fact that he dumped his victims in the desert area surrounding Los Angeles, California, Glatman's victims had no obvious relationship to one another. It turned out, after investigation, that most of the victims had either needed cash or were interested in modeling careers at the time of their death. Glatman met them by responding to their personal ads in the newspaper and by posting ads of his own, posing as a legitimate magazine photographer.

Although a killer's victims may not look alike, live in the same neighborhood, or share other obvious features, an investigation that includes interviews with their family and friends might reveal an important link between seemingly unrelated murders, such as Glatman's victims. It might also reveal the motivation of the killer and his method of finding victims. What a profiler knows about the victims of a serial offender can also help citizens protect themselves. If the offender seems to be targeting college women who walk home from campus after dark, for example, students can be warned and advised not to walk alone at night. Unfortunately, it is not always possible to protect everyone from danger—especially when a serial killer is not afraid of being caught by police.

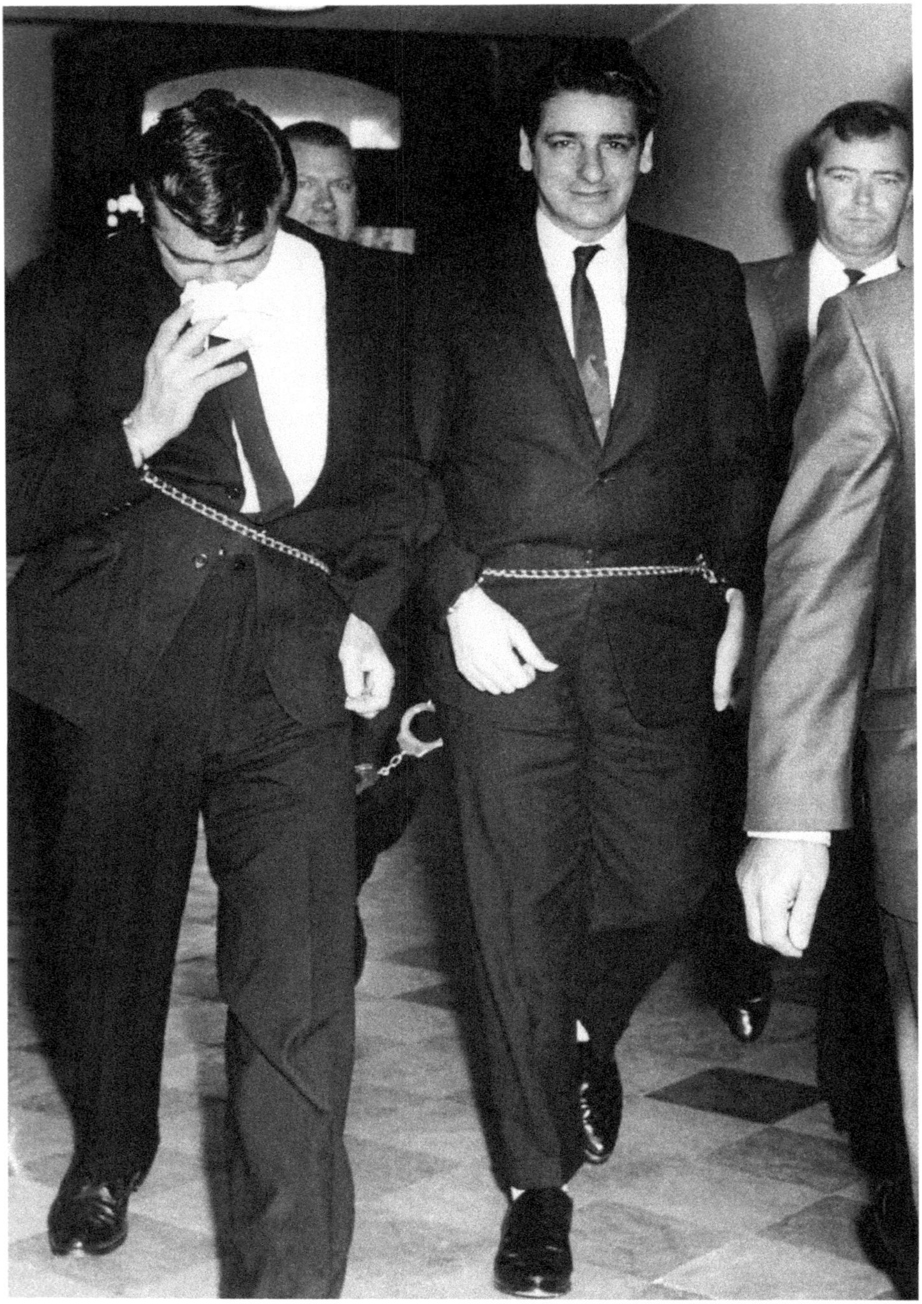

Albert DeSalvo (center) tied a piece of clothing in a bow under his victims' chins. It is believed that the victims—all women—voluntarily let him in because they either knew him or thought he was a repairman.

When violent murderer Peter Kurten was captured in Germany after a string of grisly killings in the 1920s, he stated at his trial, "I did not kill either people I hated, or people I loved. I killed whoever crossed my path at the moment my urge for murder took hold of me."[33] Kurten's statement about what motivated him to kill shows just how frightening, unpredictable, and hard to catch such a person can be. For experienced profilers, though, there is almost always a link to be found between victim and killer. After all, in one way or another, the two spent time together. An investigation into the background of a victim will often tie in to the identity of the offender, if the profiler is skilled enough to find the connection.

Chapter Four
Into the Mind of the Murderer

Offender profiling is based on the idea that the characteristics of the killer can be determined through examining the characteristics of the crime. It uses evidence found at the crime scene, victim and witness accounts, and any details about the killer's behavior to create a profile of the type of person who would commit this crime. It is different from conventional detective work because it does not point to a specific individual, but instead shows the probability of a person with certain behaviors to commit certain types of crimes.

Peter B. Ainsworth, an expert in criminal profiling, identified four approaches to offender profiling in his book *Offender Profiling and Crime Analysis*. The geographical approach examines the time and location of the murders to determine where the suspects may live and work. Investigative psychology uses widely accepted psychological theories to predict the murderer's behavior. The typological approach categorizes the offender based on clues from the crime scenes, and the clinical approach is used to help determine whether or not the killer has a mental or psychological abnormality.

David V. Canter is a profiler who was instrumental in helping to capture serial rapist and murderer John Duffy in London, England, in the 1980s. He argued that a criminal

> *leaves* psychological *traces, tell-tale patterns of behaviour that indicate the sort of person he is … They cannot be taken into a laboratory and dissected under the microscope. They are more like shadows which undoubtedly are connected to the criminal who cast*

them, but they flicker and change, and it may not always be obvious where they come from. Yet, if they can be fixed and interpreted, a criminal's shadows can indicate where investigators should look and what sort of person they should be looking for.[34]

Gathering the Facts

Profiling a criminal begins first with the facts: what, where, and how something was done, and to whom. Profilers want every bit of evidence police have in a case, because at first, their profession demands that they assume nothing. Instead, they use the facts to reconstruct the crime scene and narrow down exactly what happened. This is an example of deductive reasoning, or looking at known facts to conclude what the criminal has done. Deductive reasoning is essential to the profiling process because it helps answer the question of why the criminal did this thing, in this way, in this place, on this day, and to this person. Deductive reasoning after gathering the facts in the case leads a profiler to an offender's motive—what drove them to commit a certain crime. Was it revenge? Was it for profit? Was it totally random? When the profiler has seen all the available evidence in a case and has deduced what the offender did, the m.o., and the motive (why the crime was committed), it is time to make some educated guesses about the offender.

Deducing what happened is part of any criminal investigation and any profile, and it involves the advice of many different experts in criminal investigations. Inductive reasoning, or making educated guesses about what kind of person the offender is, is based on research and experience. Profilers make their living studying different kinds of crimes, and more importantly, the different kinds of people who commit them. This background is critical to pinpointing the specific facts in a case that reflect the offender's behavior and important personal traits.

Much of profiling is based on recognizing patterns. A profiler looks at all the facts of a particular case to decide which characteristics of that case point to characteristics of the person who committed the crime. These guesses are based partly on the details of similar crimes that have been committed in the past and partly on knowledge of human behavior. Using their vast knowledge about previous cases and about how criminals think, profilers induce, or guess, what kind of person would do the things that were done at a particular crime scene.

Inductive reasoning includes the use of statistics: If most serial killers in a certain country are between the ages of 25 and 35, for example, then a

Controversy in Profiling

Racial profiling is a very controversial topic in law enforcement around the globe. Reports of traffic stops and police arrests in cities across the United States show that minority citizens are far more likely than whites to be questioned by police for a variety of offenses. There is a difference, however, between criminal profiling and racial profiling. Racial profiling targets suspects of a particular crime based on their race, ethnicity, national origin, or religion. Criminal profiling identifies likely characteristics of a suspect based on their behavior during a specific crime or set of crimes. While it is impossible to ignore race when creating a criminal profile, basing a profile on generalizations instead of the specific behavior of the criminal could lead to the wrong pool of suspects, which is devastating to a criminal investigation.

To combat the problem of racial profiling, many police departments provide training in the difference between bias-based profiling and criminal profiling. The use of video cameras in patrol cars and police body cameras is another way to ensure that the officers' interactions with minority suspects are professional.

profiler would consider this probability in deciding the age of a particular killer in question. If profilers used only inductive reasoning, however, anyone with a computer and access to crime databases could be a profiler. Profiling is much more complicated than looking at statistics—profilers use both inductive and deductive reasoning to come to a conclusion.

Additionally, inductive reasoning is not generally based on a single case; inductive assumptions are broad generalizations that can apply to many cases. Although profilers do depend on statistics from past cases to a certain extent, these general facts are no replacement for the skills, experience, and instinct a profiler can bring to each individual, unsolved case.

As an experienced criminal profiler works with both inductive and deductive reasoning, they are able to tie both kinds of assumptions together to create the specific profile of the serial criminal under investigation.

By the Numbers

113

the average intelligence quotient (IQ) of serial killers

Organization of the Offender

Just as crime scenes are classified as disorganized or organized, so are the offenders who leave these kinds of scenes behind. In crimes of serial rape and murder, which make up the bulk of most profilers' caseloads, deciding whether the offender is organized or not allows a profiler to make other very important predictions—everything from where an offender lives and works to what kind of vehicle they drive and what kind of student they may have been in school. Important components and considerations in a criminal profile are an offender's history, their personality, their physical attributes, and their habits.

Disorganized criminals tend to leave behind messy crime scenes with a lot of physical evidence. From this, profilers conclude that the criminal acted on the spur of the moment. Little planning went into the crime, and the offender did little to clean up after their crime, leaving fingerprints, footprints, the weapon, and other kinds of evidence out in the open. From the details of a disorganized crime scene, profilers may suspect certain details about the offender. Statistically, they are likely to have below-average intelligence and poor social skills. A profiler would combine details such as these with features of the crime scene to give police investigators a far more useful description of the person they should be looking for.

When a young woman named Betty Jane Shade was killed in Pennsylvania in 1979 and her body was dumped at an illegal trash site, John E. Douglas, the profiler on the case, recognized clear signs of a disorganized offender and gave police some information that helped them narrow down their suspects. "I thought they should be looking for a white male, aged seventeen to twenty-five," Douglas explained. "He would be thin or wiry, a loner, not exactly a whiz kid in high school." He also gave details about the killer's probable personality, home life, and type of job: "I told the police not to look for the 'used-car salesman type down

Disorganized criminals leave behind messy crime scenes, giving profilers clues about their personalities; sometimes, they even leave the weapon behind.

3
4

Forensic Science

Forensic science plays a huge part in any criminal investigation. Thorough examination of the evidence at the crime scene answers many questions about the criminal and their behavior. The Denver Crime Lab at the Colorado Bureau of Investigation analyzes evidence in cases all over the state. Their departments include:

Fingerprints and impressions (from shoes, tires, and more): This department processes fingerprints and impressions, running them through a national database and comparing them with millions of other fingerprints.

Trace evidence: This unit identifies and compares substances such as paint, glass, or dirt.

Chemistry: These forensic scientists analyze and compare drugs, explosives, or unknown chemicals.

Computer crimes: This unit retrieves evidence from computers, improves audio or video evidence, and analyzes this data.

Firearms and toolmark identification: This department identifies and tests guns to establish patterns and entry angles, as well as to compare bullets and casings.

Serology and DNA: These scientists analyze bodily fluids or hair for identification.

Questioned documents: This department investigates forgery crimes, compares handwriting, and reconstructs documents relevant to a crime scene.

the street with the outgoing personality' ... Anyone who would leave the body at that sort of dump site had to have a menial job or something that involved dirt or grime."[35]

Ultimately, it turned out that there were two killers, one of which was Shade's boyfriend. The killers were brothers, both from the kind of family background Douglas had predicted, and they worked as trash haulers, the kind of job he also predicted. They also fit the age group and personality type of the profile, more so than the other suspects police had in mind. The brothers were arrested and convicted of Shade's murder in a case that showed how the profile of a disorganized offender, even when slightly off target, can put murderers behind bars before they strike again.

The Intelligent, Socially Skilled Killer

Organized criminals leave behind different kinds of crime scenes, ones that show a good deal of planning and point to an offender who is both intelligent and socially skilled. When profilers see organized crime scenes, they recognize an offender who targets their victims and covers their tracks. Inductive reasoning tells them they may be dealing with someone who lives an otherwise normal life and might even be married and have a family. It is likely that the person not only will commit more crimes, but will also get better at not getting caught.

"The organized offender often uses a ruse or a con to gain control over his victim," explained Robert K. Ressler. "This is a man who has good verbal skills and a high degree of intelligence, enough to lure the victim into a vulnerable area."[36] Because organized offenders plan their crimes, the offender often spends time figuring out how to trick their victims. "With the organized killer," Ressler wrote, "the offender has enough verbal and other interchange with the victims to recognize them as individuals prior to killing them."[37] This type of information often helps profilers create a picture of an intelligent person who acts friendly and then snares their victims.

When two criminals, later nicknamed the Railway Killers, began committing rapes near railroad tracks in London in 1982, the early victims described a man whose friendly conversation had put them off guard long enough for him to attack. He then threatened them with a knife while committing the rape. In 1985, the rapists escalated to murder, strangling one victim. They went on to murder others, and the frustrated London police asked a behavioral science professor, David Canter, to create a psychological profile of the killer.

Canter used statistical analysis and victimology, combined with his experience and skill, to create a profile that estimated the killer (or killers) lived in northwestern London, could be married, and probably had a history of violence. Applying the details of Canter's profile to their huge group of suspects, the list was quickly narrowed down from around 2,000 suspects to just 1: John Duffy.

"Canter's profile proved accurate in thirteen of its seventeen points," explained one expert. "Particularly perceptive was his suggestion that the killer was childless;

Seward Hwy
RIGHT LANE MUST TURN RIGHT
KIA
OPEN

Israel Keyes abducted one of his victims, Samantha Koenig, from the coffee shop shown here. After killing her, he demanded ransom payments, pretending she was still alive. Regarded as one of the most organized serial killers, Keyes would murder his victims in remote locations, then take the corpses with him and bury them in another state. He stashed crime kits across the country containing money, weapons, and other tools he needed to commit his murders.

Firestarters

Arsonists are difficult to profile because they have numerous motives, and relatively few have been arrested and interviewed. However, profilers over the years have collected enough data to form a standard set of attributes for arsonists. These are some common characteristics of arsonists:

Age: 17 to 26
Gender: male
Race: white
Social status: has a low-paying job; working class
Home life: unstable childhood, abusive parents
Social life: lack of stable relationships, socially awkward
Mental health: common diagnoses are schizophrenia, personality disorders, or substance abuse
Other: obsession with firefighting, record of poor military performance

this had, apparently, been a great source of anguish to Duffy."[38] Before the profile, the Railway Killers (Duffy had enlisted the help of a friend for many of the crimes) had been impossible for the police to positively identify and track down. The case served as a powerful example of using criminal profiling to capture extremely dangerous organized serial killers.

Other Serial Crimes

Putting serial killers such as Duffy behind bars is one of the great rewards of profiling, but not all profiled offenders are rapists or murderers. A profiler's skills may be put to use in solving any kind of criminal puzzle.

Serial arsonists and bombers work much differently than an organized serial rapist or a violent, disorganized murderer. A person who sets fires may not even mean to hurt anyone, although the crimes may lead to deaths if fires are set in buildings where people live or work. A serial bomber who wants to send a political message rather than kill may commit crimes from a considerable distance, and unlike other kinds of killers, they may never actually see the faces of the victims at all.

Although they work differently than the rapists and murderers who make up many of a profiler's cases, arsonists and bombers frequently also have some sort of psychological imbalance, and this makes them prime targets for a profiler's skills. Reading the behavioral clues of these criminals' actions, profilers may be able to point police in the exact direction of the arsonist or bomber they seek.

An Explosive Delivery

For decades, beginning in the 1970s, a serial bomber terrorized U.S. citizens by mailing explosives to people. During his reign as one of America's most notorious criminals, this serial bomber targeted mostly university professors, which gave him his infamous nickname: the Unabomber. Before he was finally caught in 1996, he had killed 3 people and seriously injured more than 20 others.

To help catch the criminal at the heart of what was, at the time, one of the most expensive and expansive criminal investigations in U.S. history, the FBI sent profilers to work on the case. In 1993, the *New York Times* printed the details of the FBI's profile. Reporter Stephen Labaton wrote that federal investigators believed the bomber was "an obsessive-compulsive white man who was [raised] in the Chicago area and probably has had menial jobs ... To re-live the experience, he probably keeps souvenirs like newspaper clippings and videotapes."[39] In a 2017 National Public Radio interview with case profiler James R. Fitzgerald, he stated that they were able to figure out where the Unabomber was from because of an article he wrote—there were terms and regional language of the Chicago, Illinois, area, and the first bombs were either mailed from or placed around Chicago. Additionally, profilers predicted that the bomber was the type to visit the scene of his crimes to watch the parcel blow up.

When investigators finally tracked the Unabomber down, the man behind the nickname—Ted Kaczynski—did indeed fit many details of the profile. He was born in Chicago, and he was in his 30s when the bombings began. When his small Montana cabin was examined for evidence after his capture, police found it packed from floor to ceiling with "souvenirs" collected during half a lifetime of bombings. Ultimately, however, the FBI's criminal profile was not the piece of the investigation that directly led to the Unabomber's capture. Profiling expert John E. Douglas argued that by the time the profile was created, Kaczynski was already well into his criminal career and had become much more skilled at getting away. "Most of these guys are catchable early in their careers," he wrote, "before they start perfecting what they do and moving around the country." Having worked

The Unabomber, Ted Kaczynski, was finally captured not because of a criminal profile, but because his brother recognized Kaczynski's writing style in a document published in a newspaper.

on the Unabomber profile himself, Douglas claimed that "had we been where we are now with profiling in 1979, Unabomber might have been caught years earlier."[40]

Heated Profiling

Arsonists, similarly to bombers, typically leave a pattern of behavior behind that a profiler can use to identify them. In 2005, restaurant manager Thomas A. Sweatt was arrested for setting fire to dozens of homes and apartments around Washington, D.C. The profile created to help find him determined, based on his tactic of leaving gasoline-filled jugs on front porches and lighting them with wicks so he would have enough time to sneak away, that he was a person with a deceptive personality—

One of the most notable arsonists in Los Angeles, California, history was former fire captain John Leonard Orr. He is believed to have started more than 2,000 fires in the Los Angeles area in the 1980s.

someone who would seem to his coworkers and neighbors like a very nice person.

After his arrest, his neighbors claimed that he seemed normal, happy, and certainly not like a criminal. Arsonists, like other serial criminals, generally have a signature behavior and a consistent m.o., making them prime candidates for criminal profiling. However, arson is not always used to murder people. Often, an arsonist is simply obsessed with fire. Experts believe that arsonists are less likely to want to commit violence and more likely to have a significant psychological disorder. Arson may be a future serial killer's introduction to crime. Murderer David Berkowitz, whose killing spree of teenagers in the 1970s earned him the nickname Son of Sam, confessed that he had started hundreds of small fires in New York City in the years before he escalated to murder.

A history of setting fires, like a history of torturing animals, signals to profilers that a person may be headed toward a life of the worst kinds of crimes. This is why many profilers predict details of an offender's childhood when they create a profile of a serial criminal. Some of the cases in which childhood plays a particularly important role to the profile are those in which the predicted killer does not fit the typical profile of a serial murderer—instead of being a man aged 25 to 35, the killer is a woman.

Wicked Women

The most notorious and infamous serial killers—such as Jack the Ripper, John Wayne Gacy, Ted Bundy, and Jeffrey Dahmer—fit the traditional profile of a murderer, including the fact that they were all men. The vast majority of serial killers are men. For this reason, criminal profilers on the hunt for deadly killers typically predict that offenders are male.

Nonetheless, there are female serial killers. Often, they just commit their crimes in different ways. Rarely are their deeds especially gruesome—at least, not in a bloody sense. They almost never torture their victims or mutilate the bodies the way many male killers do. Instead, women killers commonly hide their crimes by choosing people who are very sick or very old—helpless victims whose death will not come as much of a surprise to others. The murder weapons of female serial killers are not generally knives or guns, but bottles and pillows. They prefer to poison their victims or smother them to death, choosing an m.o. that leaves little or no evidence behind. Especially when they have jobs as caretakers of helpless people, these criminals

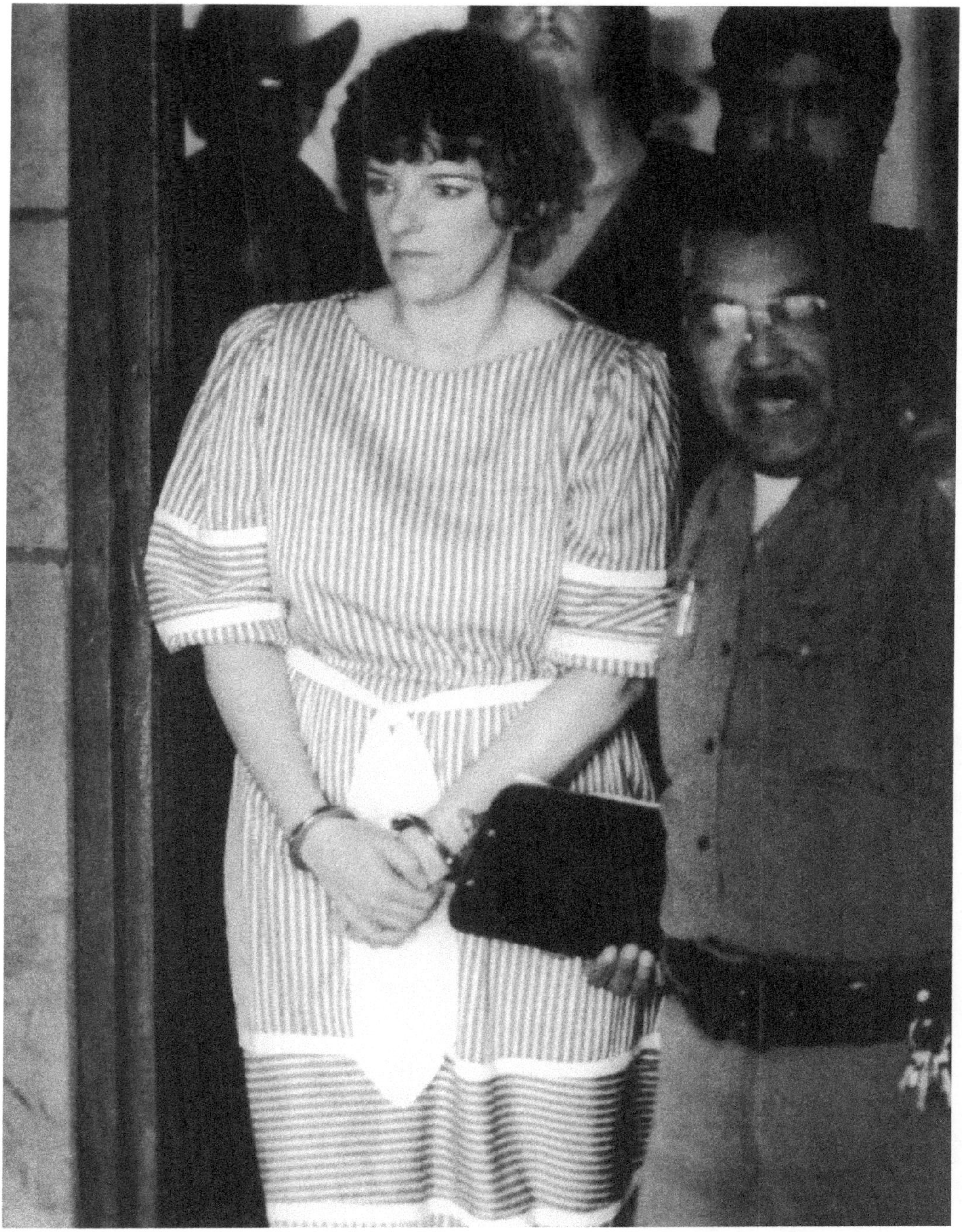

Genene Jones, nicknamed the Angel of Death, enjoyed creating medical emergencies in order to help during them. This is a trait that might be analyzed by a criminal profiler.

can remain in one place, killing quite often, and not be suspected of murder because their victims are people who were expected to die soon of natural causes. Therefore, no one realizes that the cause of death was actually homicide.

"There are no marks or other types of evidence to examine, making detection quite difficult," author Deborah Schurman-Kauflin wrote. "The pattern appears to be: many deaths surrounding one lone female caregiver."[41] The process of profiling a female serial killer is different from profiling a male. This is because female killers are relatively easy to catch once someone catches on to them. They often live or work in the very place where they commit most of their murders. The challenge is figuring out that the deaths (in a nursing home, for example) were not of natural causes. Once this is determined, the suspect list will probably be small, and one caregiver will stand out among the rest as the person with a connection to all the deaths.

Schurman-Kauflin claimed that female killers tend to be high-school dropouts who are younger than 30. They commonly played alone as children because they never fit in. Female serial killers often have a history of acne and weight problems, especially when they were teenagers, and they are often fascinated by death and torture. Creating a profile of characteristics such as these can help the investigation, even when police have a suspect. "A good profiler can construct an effective investigative and interview strategy," Schurman-Kauflin wrote. "The ... characteristics may help narrow a field of suspects and provide insight into a killer's mind. This is what profiling is all about."[42]

One of the most infamous female serial killers was Genene Jones, a nurse in San Antonio, Texas, who is suspected of killing dozens of infants by injecting them with drugs that caused heart attacks and breathing problems. Investigators believe her motive was simply enjoying the thrill of helping during the emergencies that resulted from her injections, as hospital staff members desperately tried to revive the babies, many of whom died in spite of their efforts.

"In order to estimate why an offender engages in certain behaviors," Schurman-Kauflin wrote, "there must be an understanding of what emotional state dominates the individual who commits the crime."[43] Experts believe that Jones's actions may have resulted in the deaths of more than 60 children. In 1984, she was sentenced to 160 years in prison for her string of horrific crimes. She was still being charged with murder for more deaths in 2017, and prosecutors are fighting against her 2018 early release date. She is proof that the terrifying cases demanding the expertise of a criminal profiler can take countless different forms, but they all depend on a profiler's ability to read crimes of all kinds and analyze the people who commit them.

Chapter Five
"Yours, Truly Guiltily"

Dennis Rader, a serial killer known as BTK (Bind, Torture, Kill), signed his first letter to the public "yours, truly guiltily."[44] He described his first crime in January 1974: the murders of four members of the Otero family in Wichita, Kansas. The letter was found in a local library book and was published in a local newspaper in October 1974. The letter was poorly written with many grammatical errors, and its contents were chilling:

> *When this monster enter my brain, I will never know ... I can't stop it so the monster goes on, and hurt me as well as society. Society can be thankful that there are ways for people like me to relieve myself at time by day dreams of some victim being torture and being mine. It is a big complicated game my friend of the monster play putting victims number down, follow them, checking up on them waiting in the dark, waiting, waiting ... Maybe you can stop him. I can't. He has already chosen his next victim.*[45]

Rader's murders spanned an almost 20-year period, with a total of 10 victims. During that time, he communicated regularly with the police, once even calling them to report on himself after strangling one woman in 1977. He sent poems and letters to news stations, letting them know who had committed the crime. In his writings, he talked about other serial killers, including Ted Bundy and the Son of Sam. The killings stopped abruptly in 1991, for no known reason. The 30-year anniversary of the Otero murders in 2004 brought the BTK story back to the public eye, and Rader could not resist the spotlight. He sent the police and various news organizations letters, pictures of the

Some profilers and forensic psychologists believe Dennis Rader has many characteristics of a psychopath: He was detached, cruel, and aggressive, and he was able to keep his psychopathic personality apart from his daily life.

victims, trinkets such as jewelry taken from the victims, and even a rough draft of a book about the killings. Some of this information was given to police on a computer disk, and the police were able to trace the origin of the disk back to Rader's church, which ultimately led to his arrest.

Many high-profile serial killers send communications to law enforcement or news agencies because they want to become famous. After BTK was captured, investigators argued that Rader put himself at risk decades after committing his crimes because he wanted media attention. Profilers use any communication from the killer, whether it is a taunting message to the police or a ransom note, to learn information about their personality. Interviews, taken after murderers have been arrested, have also given profilers a wealth of insight into the mind of serial killers.

By the Numbers

15

percent of serial killer victims whose cause of death was stabbing

Conversations with a Serial Killer

"What causes a suspect to confess?" asked experienced FBI profiler Russell Vorpagel. "Why do some suspects have a need to be caught? Why do others meticulously hide their crimes? And still others have a need to toy with the police?"[46] Experts have insisted that interviews and information taken directly from killers are extremely valuable tools for profilers. Prison, in fact, was where modern profiling really took root. The first profilers officially assigned by the FBI to use psychology as a tool for tracking down offenders spent a lot of their time in prisons in the beginning of their career. They needed to compile case studies of serial criminals so they could look at details in a new case that were similar to others they had studied.

One of those earliest FBI profilers, John E. Douglas, wrote about the time he spent in prisons. "The prison visits became a regular practice," Douglas explained. "Wherever I found myself, I'd find out what prison or penitentiary was nearby and who of interest was 'in residence.'"[47] He conducted dozens of interviews, and they gave both him and his fellow profilers a stronger basis for the job they were doing.

"The more of these interviews I did,

One FBI profiler interviewed Ted Bundy (shown here) and said he felt uncomfortable about their conversations even years later. He never felt like he really understood Bundy.

An Unsolved Murder

A ransom note; a tablet of lined paper with a page of "practice" writing; a felt-tip pen used to write a ransom note found in a kitchen container: These items are some of the evidence profilers examined from the murder scene of child beauty queen JonBenét Ramsey on December 26, 1996.

John Mark Karr told police that he was at the house when JonBenét died. DNA evidence proved later that he could not be the killer, but the true murderer has never been discovered.

The note, and the "practice" draft, became the details on which much of the investigation focused. Profilers examined the note to make predictions about its author. The profiler thought the writer was a white male in his 30s or 40s; he probably had a business background, and he was almost certainly familiar with the Ramsey family. A 41-year-old white teacher named John Mark Karr confessed to JonBenét's murder in 2006, but he did not exactly match the profile. His confession was later revealed to be a hoax. Police still do not know whether the profile of the killer is accurate. As is always the case in profiling, the accuracy of a profile can only be judged when the case is solved, and JonBenét's killer was never found.

the more confident I began to feel," he wrote. "Everything had to be interpreted through hard work and extensive review on our part. What the interviews were doing, though, was letting us see the way the offender's mind worked, getting a feel for them, allowing us to start walking in their shoes."[48] Douglas's work was so pivotal and interesting that in 2017, his book *Mind Hunter: Inside the FBI's Elite Serial Crime Unit* was the basis for the Netflix series *Mindhunter*.

Profiling and Prosecution

In the decades since Douglas spent so much time conducting those early interviews, profiling has come a long way. More and more often, interviews are used to study criminals who have already been caught, narrow down suspect lists in unsolved crimes, and help police conduct the kinds of suspect interviews that will hopefully lead to a confession.

The profile of a serial criminal contains many details about the person's probable personality. Interrogations of suspects are performed in a way that is most likely to make a guilty person confess. A profiler, by looking at what the offender has done in a particular case, will be able to tell police if this is an organized or a disorganized person, as well as some of the things that are important to them. A profiler can tell police what kinds of questions to ask during the interrogation, even what time of day a confession would be most likely to come, in what kind of room, and what kinds of items should be displayed on the table, such as photos or souvenirs from the crime scenes.

When an offender is arrested and a case goes to trial, profilers sometimes help lawyers decide the best kind of questions to ask and the best witnesses to put on the stand. FBI profiler Robert K. Ressler was asked to testify in the case of Jeffrey Dahmer, who was on trial for killing at least 17 people. Surprisingly, Ressler was a defense witness who supported the defense's argument that Dahmer was insane. Dahmer was widely considered to be an organized killer—the kind commonly determined to be sane in a criminal trial. Ressler had concluded that Dahmer, at times, was disorganized in his murders.

Ressler's testimony was intended to make the insanity defense more believable when it was presented to the jury during the trial. "The idea of 'Ressler for the defense' raised eyebrows," he claimed. "But I did believe that my expertise could contribute to an understanding of the man and his crimes that would provide the necessary basis for a fair [judgment] of the case."[49]

Serial killer Jeffrey Dahmer is shown here in court. Profilers often help lawyers decide if a suspect should be put on the stand to testify and what questions should be asked.

Communication with the killers—whether during trial, in a prison interview, or by letters sent to the police or the media—is becoming more important to the process of criminal profiling. It has to be, because some offenders put communication at the very center of their crimes.

Catch Me if You Can

One of the most infamous unsolved murder cases in history is that of the Zodiac Killer. After attacking his victims, he often sent letters to or called local police to taunt them. He also sent notes to major newspapers in the San Francisco Bay Area, such as the *San Francisco Chronicle*. Whenever they got the sloppy handwritten notes, the editors knew they were hearing from the Zodiac Killer again. His was one of the most frightening killing sprees in American history, in part because the deaths and attempted murders were followed by notes and letters that threatened violence and exposed a gruesome mind.

Similarly to another killer from a century before who signed one of his own notes to the press by saying he was Jack the Ripper, the Zodiac recorded his killings with a string of correspondence. His notes were signed with a mysterious symbol: a cross over a circle.

The symbol and the nickname Zodiac became infamous, just like the nickname Jack the Ripper. Also like Jack the Ripper, the Zodiac has never been identified.

Both of these cases illustrate the perverse need of some killers to communicate with police and the media. Like both the Ripper and the Zodiac, some serial criminals taunt police with insults or challenges, and their letters generally hold the frightening promise of more violence to come. For profilers, communication like this can both help and harm a case. It is helpful because it is a strong behavioral clue. The need to communicate tells profilers a great deal about a criminal's frame of mind and why they feel the need to broadcast their crimes.

Correspondence can also make profiling much more challenging, however, because of copycats: people who also write letters pretending to be the killer. Then, profilers have the added challenge of deciding which letters are really from the killer and which might be fakes. In the case of the Zodiac, investigators knew the killer's letters were authentic because he discussed crime details that police had not released, including information only the person who committed the murders could have known.

The author of Jack the Ripper's

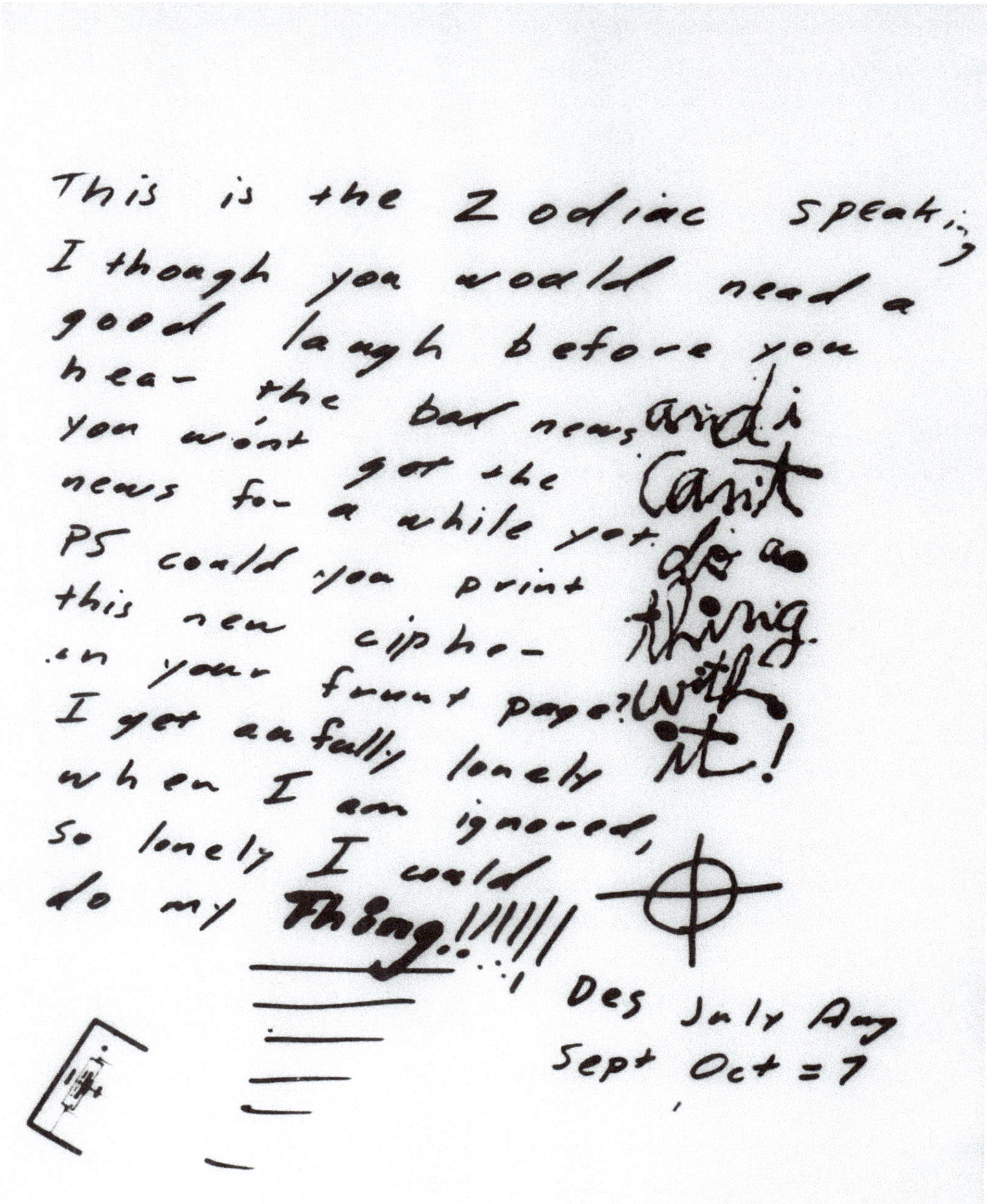

This is the Zodiac speaking
I though you would need a good laugh before you hear the bad news you wont get the news for a while yet.
PS could you print this new cipher in your frunt page? I get awfully lonely when I am ignored, so lonely I could do my Thing!!!!!!
and i cant do a thing with it!
Des July Aug Sept Oct = 7

The Zodiac Killer sent many letters, including the one shown here, to newspapers such as the San Francisco Chronicle. *The letters were signed with a cross over a circle and threatened more violence.*

letters was not always so obvious. In fact, some modern investigators looking back on the evidence from that case suspect that the first letters might not have been written by the killer at all and that his jealousy that someone else was taking credit for his work made him respond with his own letters to the police. "When I first began to go through the Ripper letters," wrote author Patricia Cornwell, "I [agreed] with what police and most people believe: Almost all of the letters are hoaxes or the communications of mentally unbalanced people."[50] Although Cornwell goes on to say that after further study, she began to suspect that Jack the Ripper had, in fact, written most of the letters himself, her uncertainty on the matter shows just how confusing written correspondence from a criminal can be.

There are other challenges of profiling a criminal's correspondence. For example, a letter filled with misspelled words and mistakes in grammar does not always mean that its author is uneducated. A profiler might be able to determine that the words were spelled wrong on purpose to make police believe that the criminal is illiterate or comes from another country. Such a letter might be designed to throw investigators off the trail, but it may in fact lead a profiler in a different direction. To the profiler, such a letter could point to a very educated person, perhaps even one who speaks several languages. The offender's efforts might backfire, perhaps helping profilers narrow down the suspect list to highly educated people.

All correspondence that criminals have with police can help solve a case, but sometimes, letters are the entire key to preventing a murder from happening in the first place. These cases are kidnappings for ransom, and a profiler's skills at reading not just the ransom note but the person who wrote it is sometimes the only hope of bringing the victim home alive.

By the Numbers

465,676

number of missing child cases in the United States in 2016

The Case of the Lindbergh Baby

In 1927, Charles Lindbergh, a former U.S. Army pilot, succeeded at something no other living person had done: He flew over the Atlantic Ocean alone in an airplane, and the feat made him

Charles Lindbergh, shown here, was a famous pilot. In 1932, his son was kidnapped.

one of the most famous and wealthy people in the United States. When Lindbergh's first child was born, the country was in the midst of the Great Depression. People were starving, and kidnapping for ransom had become a popular crime. One night in 1932, when Lindbergh's son was not even two years old, he disappeared from his nursery and was never seen alive again.

The search for the kidnapper was the biggest and most publicized case of its day. Every newspaper in the country followed the investigation. There were plenty of theories, and many fingers were pointed at Mafia gangsters. A respected psychiatrist named Dudley Shoenfeld took one look at the ransom notes the kidnapper was writing and came to a very different conclusion. The notes appeared to be written by someone with very poor spelling and terrible grammar. The first note, which the kidnapper left in the nursery in place of the baby he had taken, read, "We warn you for making anyding public or for notify the polise the child is in gute care."[51]

Most people reading such a message would immediately assume that the writer is uneducated because of the poor grammar and spelling. To Shoenfeld, however, the notes appeared to have been written by someone whose first language was not English. It was determined by translators that the notes were grammatically correct once they were translated into German, and Shoenfeld advised police that they should be looking for a German. Shoenfeld stayed with the case until the end, providing what was an early example of profiling. He predicted that the kidnapper was a fully functional, law-abiding member of society, but one who had schizophrenia. He insisted that the kidnapper acted alone, not as part of a gang.

When German-born Bruno Richard Hauptmann was arrested and put on trial for the crime, Shoenfeld still acted the part of the profiler in a time when no such profession existed. He attended the trial, giving advice to prosecutors about how to question Hauptmann on the stand. In the hopes of gathering data, Shoenfeld asked that Hauptmann not receive the death penalty if he was found guilty, so profilers could study his mind. Hauptmann was convicted of both kidnapping and murdering the Lindbergh baby; he was put to death. Still, Shoenfeld made history by profiling Hauptmann's characteristics from his written communication, and he helped establish the modern role of the profiler—not just the important task of tracking down an offender, but also in assisting at trials and studying

Bruno Richard Hauptmann's case is sometimes seen as an example of biased profiling because after World War I, the United States and Germany were bitter enemies. Bias has long been a criticism of criminal profiling, and some people question Hauptmann's guilt.

convicts to learn about the workings of a criminal mind.

Criminal Profiling, Criminal Science

Despite the fact that the FBI has used profiling since the 1970s, it is still considered a relatively new field in the world of criminology, and it has its fair share of critics. Because it cannot be considered an exact science, many criminal justice experts and researchers are demanding more independent, unbiased studies be done to verify the accuracy of profiling. Very little such research has been done in the past because of the inaccessibility of FBI case files.

Many experts in the mental health field also question the usefulness of the FBI profiling system. Psychologists argue that the entire system was developed by people who were not trained psychologists. Profiling has come a very long way since its early days of guesswork, however, and some psychologists have been working to refine and improve the process. David Canter is one of the founders of the field of investigative psychology, and he has argued that it is crucial in offender profiling. While the goals of offender profiling and FBI profiling are the same, the difference is investigative psychologists base their predictions off of peer reviewed research instead of the personal experience of criminal investigators.

For example, Canter conducted studies on the FBI's organized and disorganized serial murderer profiles and has concluded that almost all murders are organized to some degree. He concluded that the difference lies in examining the kind of disorganized behaviors evident at the crime scene and that serial murderers should be categorized based on their interaction with the victim. Canter argued these studies based on scientific methods are the only way to develop reliable information about the behavior of serial killers.

In the 1990s, forensic psychologist Richard Kocsis developed a profiling model based on analyses of serial murders, rape, and arson. This system, called Crime Action Profiling (CAP) was designed based on the interviews given by clinical psychiatrists to establish diagnoses in their patients. CAP models give information about location, demographics, and psychological predictors of unknown suspects based on the clinical knowledge of forensic psychologists, psychiatrists, and criminologists.

While Kocsis and Canter both believe that scientific research is the root of criminal profiling, Kocsis also recognizes that the quality of the profile also lies in the ability of the profiler

Speculation and Evidence

Criminal profiles involve a lot of guesswork, and for that reason they are typically not used by prosecutors in criminal trials. A profile might indeed lead police to the right suspect, but then it is up to police to establish the trail of hard evidence linking that person to the crime. In some cases, however, a profile has become part of that trail of hard evidence. In one case in Delaware in 1989, a profile helped police track down the killer of two young women because it described an offender who would drive a van with high mileage and who would find his victims by cruising the streets. A female officer was assigned to work undercover to bait the offender. A man who fit the profile did indeed pick her up. Carpet fibers from his van matched those found on the two victims, and police arrested the driver. The court admitted the profile as evidence at the trial, deciding that a criminal profile creates probable cause to search a suspect's belongings.

and even admits that his CAP model is far from perfect. When asked if profiling is either an art or a science, most educated experts would agree that it is a combination of both.

Whether it is considered a science or not, there is little argument that criminal profiling has been instrumental in solving some difficult serial murder cases. Despite their difficulties in the past, the FBI now employs forensic psychologists. The combination of the investigative experience of law enforcement and the clinical research of mental health professionals has been a great contribution to the field of criminal profiling. While their approaches may be very different, their goal is the same: putting dangerous criminals behind bars before they strike again.

Notes

Introduction: Criminal Profiling—Linking Evidence, Behavior, and Crime

1. Quoted in Malcolm Gladwell, "Dangerous Minds: Criminal Profiling Made Easy," *The New Yorker*, November 12, 2007. www.newyorker.com/magazine/2007/11/12/dangerous-minds.

2. Quoted in John Douglas and Mark Olshaker, *Mindhunter: Inside the FBI's Elite Serial Crime Unit*. New York, NY: Simon & Schuster, 1998. PDF e-book.

Chapter One: The Art of Criminal Profiling

3. Quoted in Lea Winerman, "Criminal Profiling: The Reality Behind the Myth," *American Psychological Association*, July/August 2004.

4. Gregg O. McCrary, *The Unknown Darkness: Profiling the Predators Among Us*. New York, NY: HarperCollins, 2004, p. 11.

5. McCrary, *The Unknown Darkness*, p. 12.

6. McCrary, *The Unknown Darkness*, p. 30.

7. McCrary, *The Unknown Darkness*, p. 24.

8. John E. Douglas, Robert K. Ressler, Ann W. Burgess, and Carol R. Hartman, "Criminal Profiling from Crime Scene Analysis," in *Profilers: Leading Investigators Take You Inside the Criminal Mind*, John H. Campbell and Don DeNevi, eds. Amherst, NY: Prometheus, 2004, p. 16.

9. Deborah Schurman-Kauflin, *The New Predator: Women Who Kill: Profiles of Female Serial Killers*. New York, NY: Algora, 2000, pp. 137, 179.

10. Douglas et al., "Criminal Profiling," p. 17.

11. Schurman-Kauflin, *The New Predator*, p. 217.

12. Katherine Ramsland, *The Forensic Psychology of Criminal Minds*. New York, NY: Penguin, 2010. PDF e-book.

13. Ramsland, *Forensic Psychology*, PDF e-book.

14. McCrary, *The Unknown Darkness*, p. 11.

15. Mary Ellen O'Toole, "Criminal Profiling: The FBI Uses Criminal Investigative Analysis to Solve Crimes," in *Profilers: Leading Investigators Take You Inside the Criminal Mind*, John H. Campbell and Don DeNevi, eds. Amherst, NY: Prometheus, 2004, p. 224.

16. Douglas et al., "Criminal Profiling," pp. 17–18.

17. D. Kim Rossmo, "Geographic Profiling Update," in *Profilers: Leading Investigators Take You Inside the Criminal Mind*, John H. Campbell and Don DeNevi, eds. Amherst, NY: Prometheus, 2004, p. 295.

Chapter Two: Crime Scene Analysis

18. Quoted in Katherine Ramsland, "Are you Profiling, Profiling, or Profiling?," *Psychology Today*, December 2, 2012. www.psychologytoday.com/blog/shadowboxing/201212/are-you-profiling-profiling-or-profiling.

19. Rossmo, "Geographic Profiling Update," p. 300.

20. Russell Vorpagel, *Profiles in Murder: An FBI Legend Dissects Killers and Their Crimes*. As told by Joseph Harrington. New York, NY: Dell, 1998, p. 34.

21. Schurman-Kauflin, *The New Predator*, pp. 141–142.

22. Robert K. Ressler and Ann W. Burgess, "Classifying Sexual Homicide Crime Scenes: Interrater Reliability," in *Profilers: Leading Investigators*

Take You Inside the Criminal Mind, John H. Campbell and Don DeNevi, eds. Amherst, NY: Prometheus, 2004, p. 95.

23. Brent Turvey, *Criminal Profiling: An Introduction to Behavioral Evidence Analysis*. San Diego, CA: Academic Press, 2002, pp. 229–230.

24. Turvey, *Criminal Profiling*, pp. 324–325.

25. Douglas and Olshaker, *Mindhunter*, PDF e-book.

26. Rossmo, "Geographic Profiling Update," p. 299.

Chapter Three: The Victim's Story

27. Mike King and Greg Cooper, *Cold Case Investigations*. San Clemente, CA: LawTech Publishing, 2008, PDF e-book.

28. Douglas et al., "Criminal Profiling," p. 15.

29. Michael R. King, "A Multidisciplinary Approach to Solving Cold Cases," in *Profilers: Leading Investigators Take You Inside the Criminal Mind*, John H. Campbell and Don DeNevi, eds. Amherst, NY: Prometheus, 2004, p. 261.

30. O'Toole, "Criminal Profiling," p. 227.

31. Richard N. Kocsis, *Criminal Profiling: Principles and Practice*. Totowa, NJ: Humana, 2006, p. 78.

32. O'Toole, "Criminal Profiling," p. 227.

33. Quoted in Jay Robert Nash, *The Great Pictorial History of World Crime*, vol. 2. Lanham, MD: Rowman & Littlefield, 2004, p. 89.

Chapter Four: Into the Mind of the Murderer

34. Quoted in David V. Canter and Donna Youngs, *Investigative Psychology: Offender Profiling and the Analysis of Criminal Action*. West Sussex, UK: John Wiley & Sons, 2009, p. 39.

35. Douglas and Olshaker, *Mindhunter*, PDF e-book.

36. Robert K. Ressler, "How to Interview a Cannibal," in *Profilers: Leading Investigators Take You Inside the Criminal Mind*, John H. Campbell and Don DeNevi, eds. Amherst, NY: Prometheus, 2004, p. 138.

37. Ressler, "Cannibal," p. 138.

38. Colin Evans, *The Casebook of Forensic Detection: How Forensic Science Solved 100 of the World's Most Baffling Crimes*. New York, NY: Berkley Books, 2007. PDF e-book.

39. Stephen Labaton, "Portrait of a Serial Bomber Emerges After Parcel Blasts," *New York Times*, June 26, 1993. www.nytimes.com/1993/06/26/us/portrait-of-a-serial-bomber-emerges-after-parcel-blasts.html.

40. Douglas and Olshaker, *Mindhunter*, PDF e-book.

41. Schurman-Kauflin, *The New Predator*, p. 18.

42. Schurman-Kauflin, *The New Predator*, pp. 181, 217.

43. Schurman-Kauflin, *The New Predator*, p. 179.

Chapter Five: "Yours, Truly Guiltily"

44. Quoted in Carlton Smith, *The BTK Murders: Inside the "Bind, Torture, Kill" Case that Terrified America's Heartland*. New York, NY: St. Martin's Press, 2006, p. 298.

45. Quoted in Stephen Singular, *Unholy Messenger: The Life and Crimes of the BTK Serial Killer*. New York, NY: Pocket Books, 2006, p. 81.

46. Vorpagel and Harrington, *Profiles in Murder*, p. 102.

47. Douglas and Olshaker, *Mindhunter*, PDF e-book.

48. Douglas and Olshaker, *Mindhunter*, PDF e-book.

49. Ressler, "Cannibal," p. 146.

50. Patricia Cornwell, *Portrait of a Killer: Jack the Ripper—Case Closed*. New York, NY: Berkley, 2002. PDF e-book.

51. Quoted in John Olsson and June Luchjenbroers, *Forensic Linguistics*. London, UK: Bloomsbury, 2014, p. 79.

For More Information

Books

Behnke, Allison. *Racial Profiling: Everyday Inequality*. Minneapolis, MN: Twenty-First Century Books, 2017.
Criminal profiling is sometimes abused and used for discriminatory practices; this title outlines how racial profiling, one way of abusing criminal psychology, affects lives.

Campbell, John H., and Don Denevi. *Profilers: Leading Investigators Take You Inside The Criminal Mind*. Amherst, NY: Prometheus Books, 2004.
Experts in homicide and criminal profiling share how they found notorious serial killers such as Jeffrey Dahmer and the Unabomber in this book.

Cannell, Michael. *Incendiary: The Psychiatrist, the Mad Bomber, and the Invention of Criminal Profiling*. New York, NY: Minotaur Books, 2017.
This book features details on the history of criminal profiling, as well as insights into the Mad Bomber case.

Navarro, Joe, and Toni Sciarra Poynter. *Dangerous Personalities: An FBI Profiler Shows You How to Identify and Protect Yourself from Harmful People*. New York, NY: Rodale Books, 2014.
In this book, a former FBI profiler describes how to identify characteristics in people with certain personality disorders that may be potentially dangerous.

Ramsland, Katherine. *The Forensic Psychology of Criminal Minds*. New York, NY: Berkley Publishing Group, 2010.
This fascinating book showcases the differences between reality and the fiction of crime shows such as *Criminal Minds* and delves into the facts of some of the real-life cases that inspired episodes of the show.

Websites

Crime Museum
(**www.crimemuseum.org/crime-library/serial-killers**)
This website presents information about types of serial killers, how they choose their victims, and specific details about the most infamous serial killers and how they were captured.

Crime Traveller
(**www.crimetraveller.org**)
This website includes case files of criminals and statistics on crime research and the criminal mind.

Criminal Profiling
(**www.criminalprofiling.com**)
This website features news stories, FBI statistics, and links to articles about topics in profiling, including victimology and behavioral science.

"Criminal Profiling: The Reality Behind the Myth"
(**www.apa.org/monitor/julaug04/criminal.aspx**)
This informative and detailed article discusses the positives and negatives related to criminal profiling in the modern world.

Mindhunters
(**mindhuntersinc.com**)
Created by former FBI agent John E. Douglas and author Mark Olshaker, this website post links and updates regarding criminal profiling, ongoing investigations, and criminal justice.

Index

Picture Credits

Cover William Whitehurst/Corbis/Getty Images; p. 11 AP Photo/Paul Sakuma; pp. 12–13 New York Daily News Archive/Contributor/New York Daily News/Getty Images; p. 15 KAVIN LAMARQUE/Reuters/Newscom; p. 16 Print Collector/Contributor/Hulton Archive/Getty Images; pp. 18–19, 44–45 Pool/Pool/Getty Images News/Getty Images; p. 23 CBS Photo Archive/Contributor/CBS/Getty Images; p. 29 Graeme Massie/Splash News/Newscom; pp. 32, 47, 54, 73, 87, 89 Bettmann/Contributor/Bettmann/Getty Images; p. 35 Tim Boyle/Contributor/Hulton Archive/Getty Images; p. 38 Kirn Vintage Stock/Contributor/Corbis Historical/Getty Images; p. 49 AP Photo/News-Journal; pp. 50–51 Hulton Archive/Stringer/Archive Photos/Getty Images; p. 58 © iStockphoto.com/chameleonseye; pp. 60–61 NEstudio/Shutterstock.com; pp. 64–65 AP Photo/Rachel D'Oro; pp. 68–69 Stephen J. Dubner/Contributor/Hulton Archive/Getty Images; pp. 70–71 Gorb Andrii/Shutterstock.com; p. 77 AFP/Staff/AFP/Getty Images; p. 79 Bride Lane Library/Popperfoto/Contributor/Popperfoto/Getty Images; p. 80 Paula Bronstein/Staff/Getty Images News/Getty Images; pp. 82–83 Curt Borgwardt/Contributor/Sygma/Getty Images; p. 85 AP Photo.

About the Author

Christine Honders lives in upstate New York with her husband and three children. She has written over 30 books for elementary and middle school children on topics ranging from serial killers to tornadoes to cave geology. In addition, she enjoys singing jazz and swing music and performs regularly with other local musicians in her community.